Assessing Expressive Learning

*A Practical Guide for Teacher-Directed
Authentic Assessment in K–12 Visual
Arts Education*

Assessing Expressive Learning

*A Practical Guide for Teacher-Directed
Authentic Assessment in K–12 Visual
Arts Education*

Charles M. Dorn
Florida State University

Stanley S. Madeja
Northern Illinois University

F. Robert Sabol
Purdue University

LEA LAWRENCE ERLBAUM ASSOCIATES, PUBLISHERS
2004   Mahwah, New Jersey   London

Senior Acquisitions Editor:	Naomi Silverman
Editorial Assistant:	Erica Kica
Cover Design:	Gail Rubini
Cover Layout:	Kathryn Houghtaling Lacey
Textbook Production Manager:	Paul Smolenski
Text and Cover Printer:	Sheridan Books, Inc.

This book was typeset in 10.5/12 pt. Arial Roman, Bold, Italic and Condensed.
The heads were typeset in Arial Bold Condensed.

Lawrence Erlbaum Associates, Inc., Publishers
10 Industrial Avenue
Mahwah, New Jersey 07430
www.erlbaum.com

Library of Congress Cataloging-in-Publication Data

Dorn, Charles M.
Assessing expressive learning: a practical guide for teacher-directed, authentic assessment in K–12 visual arts education/Charles Dorn, Stanley Madeja, F. Robert Sabol.
  p. cm.
Includes bibliographical references and index.
ISBN 0-8058-4523-2(casebound : alk.paper)--ISBN 0-8058-4524-0 (pbk. : alk.paper)
1. Art--Study and teaching (Elementary)--United States. 2. Art--Study and teaching (Secondary)--United States. 3. Educational evaluation--United States. I. Madeja, Stanley S. II. Sabol, Frank Robert, 1949- III Title.

N353 .D67 2003
707.1´273--dc21

2002040840

Books published by Lawrence Erlbaum Associates are printed on acid-free paper, and their bindings are chosen for strength and durability.

Printed in the United States of America

10 9 8 7 6 5 4 3 2 1

To all the nation's pre-K–12 art teachers who have dedicated their best efforts to ensure that America's school children will learn to feel positively about themselves, their expressive powers and their creative abilities in art.

CHAPTER 2 ALTERNATIVE ASSESSMENT STRATEGIES FOR SCHOOLS

CHAPTER 3 THE CHARACTER OF EXPRESSIVE LEARNING AND ITS ASSESSMENT

CHAPTER 4 TEACHER TRAINING AND STUDENT PORTFOLIO ASSESSMENT

CHAPTER 5 ELECTRONIC PORTFOLIO STUDIES

CHAPTER 6 CONCLUSIONS AND RECOMMENDATIONS

Assessing Expressive Learning

*A Practical Guide for Teacher-Directed
Authentic Assessment in K–12 Visual
Arts Education*

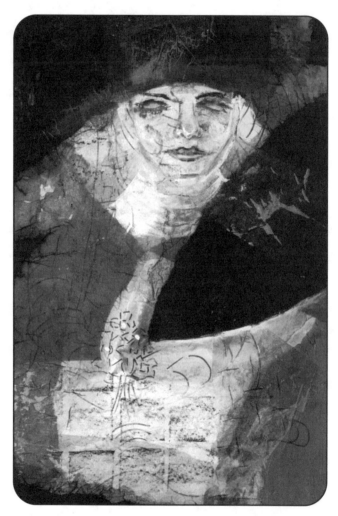

Fig. 1.1. A Mixed-media abstract drawing by a Pinellas County art teacher.

PREFACE

Assessing Expressive Learning was inspired by the concerns of its authors that thinking about and making art should remain one of the principal goals of Art Education in K–12 American schools. Furthermore, K–12 art teachers should be considered the ones most qualified to answer the question of what it is that children should know and be able to do in K–12 art as a result of their matriculation in the school art program.

Pressures from both within and outside the school in recent times have led some to question whether the goals of art learning should remain anchored to children being actively engaged in forming expressive objects of meaning or move more toward viewing the student as an active participant in an art world that makes art possible through a legitimizing theory where art is considered a production in a battleground for power struggles. What has further exacerbated this situation is efforts at national school reforms requiring the assessment of K–12 learning through standardized paper-and-pencil, true-false, and multiple choice tests.

The principal goals of this effort were, therefore, to reaffirm the notion that the artworks created by students are objects of meaning that reflect artistic valuing and aesthetic intents that provide sensory perception and appreciation because they involve elements of human motivation and interactions between the student and his or her environment. What this effort reinforces is the need for students to be involved in artistic forming where culturally differentiated experience does not contradict the universal features of art and the art experience and where psychological involvement in the work seeks to qualify the relationships between the student and the art object. Furthermore, the project was designed to support school art experiences that contribute to the enrichment of conscious life experience through providing meaning on a symbolic level and affectively through feelings that contribute to the enrichment of sensory competence and cognitive enrichment.

This text is both an effort to document an experiment where artistic values and aesthetic issues were considered paramount in the education of K–12 students in the visual arts and as a guide for the conduct of similar experiments by art teachers in the nation's schools. The report outlines both what the experimenters attempted to achieve through this approach to K–12 school art assessment and which feelings and concerns should be considered paramount and have utility for others concerned with the assessment of K–12 art learning.

With these goals in mind, the authors have attempted to provide a document that outlines the assessment procedures that were used in this study, the processes used in its evaluation, and the research evidence that supports the utility of the method. This report in no way suggests this is the only strategy that can or should be used, but rather presents a model, that if adopted, can provide an assessment process consistent with the philosophical assumptions of authentic learning.

This study was a collaborative effort by three different university researchers who, having similar goals, sought to broaden the range of the study to include studies of student, teacher, and artist attitudes toward assessment, to address the problem of quantitatively assessing student art portfolios and to search for more innovative and efficient ways to manage, store, and analyze student art portfolios, useful in the assessment of K–12 student art performance.

This book is intended to serve as a practical model that art teachers can use to accurately assess K–12 art performances using measures that can help quantify qualitative learning in ways that lend themselves to statistical analysis and to the verification of learning outcomes. Its intent is not to view artistic activity as an empirical event, but rather to demonstrate that empirical measures can be used to assess art learning in ways that are consistent with the means and ends of art. One further goal of this effort was to provide a rationale for the assessment of student art as an essential part of the K–12 instructional program and to encourage art teachers to take responsibility for and assume a leadership role in the assessment of art learning both in the school and the school district. It is envisioned that teachers following the procedures outlined in this text will gain confidence in their ability to assess their own students and the work of other teachers' students so that they can begin to develop plans for assessing student art learning in the schools.

In order to achieve these ends, art teachers must support and offer plans whereby the school's art teachers assume responsibility for the conduct of art assessment activities supported by the evidence that they are capable of carrying out that plan in the school and school district. No assessment plan would, of course, be possible without the support of the school district, including giving released time for teachers adjudicating the student work of other teachers and technical support for establishing a school-wide art student assessment plan.

Despite the helpful ideas contained in the text, there is a good deal we still need to know about how to conduct portfolio assessments in schools. Further research is needed on how to develop sampling techniques that will eliminate the need to test all students at every grade level during 12 years of schooling. We also need further experimentation with electronic imaging in the archiving of art performances electronically in order to more effectively store, manipulate, and assess electronic portfolios. In order for such studies to be successful, the nation's art teachers will need to assist in the development of alternative assessment strategies as a more efficient means for school-wide evaluation.

The project was supported by grants from the National Endowment for the Arts, the Florida Division of Cultural Affairs, and the National Art Education Association Foundation. Support also was given in the form of released time or in-service credit by four school districts, including the Pinellas County (Florida) schools, the Dade County (Florida) schools, the Washington Metropolitan (Indiana) School District, the Wayne Metropolitan (Indiana) School District, and 11 Illinois school districts. The project began in July 2000 and continued through May 2001.

Organization of the Book

The text is organized into six chapters. The introduction provides the plan of the study and its participants. Chapter 1 describes the current situation in K–12 assessment and a rationale for changes in what we need to assess. Chapter 2 describes alternative forms of assessment that need to be evaluated in school settings. Chapter 3 describes how art teachers function in the schools. Chapter 4 details the assessment and studio training processes used in the study. Chapter 5 provides a report on the applied research by teachers experimenting with the uses of electronic portfolios for assessing student art. Chapter 6 lists the findings and recommendations for further study. The Appendix lists all the supporting data.

Acknowledgments

We would like to acknowledge the assistance of a number of school personnel who organized and arranged the workshops and assisted in conducting the study, including Ray Azcuy, art supervisor of Miami-Dade County Schools; Sue Froemming, supervisor of art, Pinellas County Schools; Carol Kelly Wessel, visual arts coordinator, Washington township Public Schools; Janet Boyle, curriculum director of the Wayne Township Public Schools; and Debra C. Fitzsimmons, art teacher at Mundelein (Illinois) High School. We also thank the art teachers who braved Chicago-area snows and Miami's and St. Petersburg's summer heat to attend workshops and to collect and assess 8,000 student artworks. We also are indebted to the workshop instructors, including Louise Romeo, Dean of Art at the Miami New World School of the Arts; Pat Prisco of the Pinellas County Public Schols; Marcia Reybitz of the Dade County Schools; Joanne Caldwell and Caroline Mecklin, research assistants; Susan Uhlig of Purdue University; and Nancy Wilkerson, associate director for the Indiana Museum of Art. Moreover, a special thanks should be given to our editors and Lawrence Erlbaum Associates for publishing this work, with special mention to Naomi Silverman, Senior Editor, who saw promise in the manuscript and moved it through the review process; to reviewer David Burton of Virginia Commonwealth University, who supported the work and how it might be better organized; to Barbara Edwards, assistant to Charles Dorn, who supervised the production of the manuscript and to Gail Rubini, the graphic designer, and Katrina Ferguson, her graphic design assistant.

Charles Dorn
Stanley Madeja
F. Robert Sabol

INTRODUCTION

Assessing Expressive Learning is both a report of an effort by 70 pre-K–12 art teachers and 1,000 students in three states to participate in an authentic art assessment study and a call for school administrators and legislators to reconsider a national testing policy that supports a single set of predetermined educational standards and assessments. As a report, it attempts to chronicle the activities of these students and teachers in a year-long effort to address the problem of art assessment in pre-K–12 schooling.

The Project

Because of pressures by school administrators and state Departments of Education to regulate how art teachers assess K–12 student art performances and due to the lack of art assessment tests, opportunities for training in art assessment, and lack of information on authentic means of assessment, it was proposed that a cooperative effort by three university art education faculties and four U.S. school districts undertake the research and development of pre-K–12 art assessment models that could be replicated in the nation's schools. This effort was accomplished through three major activities: (a) teacher training and assessment development institutes, (b) applied research in school art classrooms, and (c) dissemination of the results of research to the art teaching profession. The three universities, Florida State University, Purdue University, and Northern Illinois University, who conducted the training and supervised the research, and the 11 school districts in Florida, Indiana, and Illinois participating in the project were all nationally recognized for their excellence in art teaching and learning and for their efforts to contribute their expertise to the art teaching profession as a whole. This project, which emphasizes teaching, research, and service, relates directly to the mission of all three teacher education institutions and to the needs of the school districts in meeting the demands set by national and state Goals 2000 achievement standards.

The research and development institutes focused on meeting four important needs: (a) helping teachers to understand and learn how to administer an authentic assessment model for evaluating student work in their own classes, (b) helping teachers develop an assessment plan they could adopt for use in their classrooms and schools, (c) devising a data collection system that meets the needs of the art student, and (d) meeting the school and state and national art assessment standards.

Project activities included (a) training in the use of art rubrics in assessing pre-K–12 student art performance, (b) experience in using blind scoring methods by peer teachers to validate teacher-scored student work, (c) training in the use of authentically scored student art as a curriculum tool for the improvement of art instruction, (d) the development of assessment portfolios and analytical rubrics for special needs, and (e) methods for developing assessment instruments and methods of reporting consistent with student needs and with Goals 2000 state and school district standards. The institute instructors included artists, curriculum and assessment specialists, and art teacher educators. The artists contributed the aesthetic and technical knowledge necessary for the teachers to increase their expressive abilities. This knowledge was used to assure the philosophical validity of the teachers' curriculum, which assured consistency with the means and ends of art, and provided for accurate and significant representation of the products of artistic inquiry. The curriculum and assessment specialists assisted the teachers in the writing of lesson plans, developing of rubrics and portfolios, and methods for reporting the results of assessments.

The research component of the project was conducted by project staff and statisticians who applied qualitative and quantitative research methods, descriptive statistics, and data analysis procedures to the teachers and the independent peer ratings of student art products, the methods teachers used to assess production, how assessment information was used, and how students and teachers were impacted by the classroom assessments developed by the teacher. In the evaluation of new assessment models, the researchers observed teachers and students in the schools, developed and used interview instruments, and analyzed measures of performance.

The project was a cooperative effort by three universities—Florida State University in Tallahassee, FL, Northern Illinois University in DeKalb, IL, and Purdue University in West Lafayette, IN—and the Pinellas and Dade County school districts in Florida, Washington and Wayne Township districts in Indiana and 11 school districts in Illinois. The Florida project, directed by Charles Dorn, focused mainly on the assessment of student art portfolios and on the in-service training of teachers in curriculum development and in art studio practice reported in chapter 4. The Indiana project, directed by Robert Sabol, conducted both the studio and curriculum training of teachers and, in addition, the assessment of teacher, student, and artist attitudes, as reported in chapter 1. The Illinois group, directed by Stan Madeja, focused mainly on alternative ways to develop and assess student portfolios, as reported in chapter 5.

The Florida Project

The Florida study sites included two of Florida's largest school districts, Dade (Miami) County Schools and the Pinellas (Clearwater, St. Petersburg) County Schools. The Dade County project was directed by Ray Azcuy, Dade County art supervisor, with workshops led by Louise Romeo, Dean, New World School of the Arts in Miami. The Pinellas County Schools project was directed by Sue Froemming, Pinellas County art supervisor, with workshops led by Pat Priscoe, a Pinellas County secondary art teacher. These supervisors and their districts agreed to participate in the study and also to locate between 20 and 25 teachers to volunteer to participate in the project. The teachers in both districts participated in all the training programs and portfolio adjudication sessions offered in the project.

The Illinois Project

There were two components in the Northern Illinois University project on the evaluation of expressive learning. The first component involved conducting student portfolio assessment training sessions with Illinois art teachers that paralleled the sessions in Indiana and Florida. The Illinois workshop differed from the Florida and Indiana sites in not providing studio instruction. A letter was sent to the superintendents of 11 school districts outlining the purpose of the training sessions and asking for their cooperation. Ten high school art teachers accepted the invitation to participate in the project workshops described in chapter 5. The Mundelein Schools system and Debra Fitzsimmons, a Mundelein High School art teacher, acted as school coordinator and contact person with the participating schools and art teachers. The other component was participation in the development and use of electronic portfolios as an assessment tool in high school art programs. This effort became an extension of an ongoing research study at Northern Illinois University that later expanded into a bigger project that will continue after project support ends.

Two workshops were conducted in the Illinois project. One occurred in September and the other in February, primarily to adjudicate student portfolios collected from the teachers' classes. The first workshop trained the teachers in the adjudication process, where they evaluated the portfolios of their students. In addition, the speakers gave presentations on alternative methods of assessment in the visual arts, including information on the procedures used in the Advanced Placement Studio Art Program and the International Baccalaureate programs. They also were introduced to the methodologies used to create electronic portfolios based on the Madeja model. Teachers reported on the assessment strategies used in their schools and discussed how electronic portfolios were being used as assessment tools in the school. This provided another related, but separate, component of the Illinois project, the three feasibility studies on the uses of electronic portfolios as a visual arts assessment tool at various levels of instruction. These studies are reported in more detail in chapter 5.

The Indiana Project

The institutes in Indiana included training sessions for elementary, middle, and secondary art teachers from two metropolitan school districts in Indianapolis. All the teachers were volunteers. Each had differing degrees of teaching experience and varying knowledge and training in assessing student art work. The Indiana institutes also included hands-on workshops conducted by local artists. These workshops included training in skills and techniques in figure drawing and watercolor painting. Discussions were held with the participants about the training and how they could use this knowledge in planning their curricula. Workshop discussions also included teacher reactions to the project and to issues related to the assessment of visual arts learning.

In addition to the assessment training and hands-on studio activities, the project included the presentation of a research strand that examined demographic, curriculum, instruction, assessment, attitude, and art product-related issues.

Questionnaires were created by the project director to gather input on these issues. The questionnaires were distributed to a total of 59 Florida, Indiana, and Illinois art teachers, including 472 students and 50 artists in Indiana and Florida. Separate questionnaires were created for each group. The questionnaires included closed-form, open-ended, and Likert-type items. SPSS, Version 10 software and content analysis were used to analyze data. Comparisons of responses within and across groups were done to identify similarities and differences among responses. The findings from these studies are reported in chapter 1 and in the appendixes.

Overall, 70 art teachers participated in three one- or two-day workshops held at each location. Fifty-one helped organize and participated in assessing nearly 2000 portfolios of four student artworks each. Nearly 1,000 pre-K–12 students submitted eight artworks, which provided more than 8,000 artworks to be assessed by teachers. Because each portfolio was scored by three independent raters, 24,000 independent ratings were made on student work.

Project's Rationale

With numerous school districts and state Departments of Education insisting that art teachers assess student performance, and because no art tests or school art assessment plans were forthcoming from either the state or the school districts, new approaches such as those demonstrated in this project are needed. The nation's art teachers also need to be organized to provide new directions and a new energy to school-based assessment. It is therefore believed that the nation's art teachers should begin the process of: (a) developing their own authentic assessment instruments, (b) developing school and district assessment plans using a peer review process, and (c) developing ways to document student progress and establish sensible and appropriate record-keeping systems that will meet the agreed-upon goals of the district and state.

The case for using an authentic approach in assessing K–12 art education and giving the art teacher responsibility for carrying it out in schools must be something we can demonstrate in practice. In doing so, art education professionals need to go beyond simply criticizing state-mandated one-size-fits-all paper-and-pencil tests and beyond simply complaining about state-mandated compliance and accountability measures that view students, teachers, school and school districts as competitors.

State Departments of Education who view curriculum development as a matter of regulating teachers rather than helping them regulate themselves and own their own standards are, of course, not likely to view such changes favorably. It is much easier for bureaucrats to view their primary mission as enforcing rules and mandating reforms set by politicians concerned about voter demands for drug-free schools and higher graduation standards. To trust art teachers to carry out that task would, in effect, rob them of the need to perform the very regulatory function that gives them a reason to exist. Fortunately, in the past they could count on teachers' lack of organization and distrust of testing to allow them to continue mandating meaningless true-false and multiple-choice tests, more useful in finding out which students, teachers, and schools fail rather than what makes schools better places to learn and teach.

The task of overcoming the bias of the testing community is equally daunting. Testing that takes into account different curricular goals and unequal learning environments does not provide statisticians with the necessary means for deciding who wins and who loses. The notion that tests could be used to identify how schools, students, and teachers can improve on what they are doing and how different school subjects require differing assessment strategies for assessing different forms of knowing seems alien to their thinking. How human beings differ in their interests, how they differ in the way they go about learning how things work, and how individuals choose different ways to satisfy that curiosity becomes an anathema to the test developers who want neat and tidy statistical cohorts to manipulate.

What is most needed is the hard evidence that teacher-constructed and teacher-administered tests are not only as valid and reliable as norm-referenced tests, but are even more likely to encourage schools to get better rather than be penalized for being different. In the end, we must realize that American school children are not equal in their aesthetic abilities and American schools are also not equal in the aesthetic opportunities they provide. However, if we can at least entertain the possibility that either one or both of these conditions are reversible, our best hope lies in deciding what it is that kids need to know and be able to do and making that the primary focus in reforming schools and schooling.

Organization of the Book

Chapter 1 provides a description of the current national assessment context including the impact of the standards movement, the National Assessment of Educational Progress, the role of the art teacher in the assessment process, and what art teachers know and are able to do in assessing student learning. Also addressed are the criteria used for evaluating works of art, studies of these criteria, and the attitude of art teachers and students in the project.

Chapter 2 explores several alternatives to current methods used in assessing art education in schools. These include discussion of such matters as assessment policies, the curriculum, state-wide testing programs, and the need for alternative models for assessment. Also examined are alternative methods for portfolio assessment including journals, teacher logs, controlled task investigations, and advanced placement. A description of the Madeja modeling system used in the Illinois project is also presented.

Chapter 3 discusses the expressive learning environment including the reform effort, the problem of selecting appropriate test measures, the quantification of qualitative learning, and art learning standards. Also addressed are what students in art need to know and be able to do, the most important elements of assessing expressive learning, and the development of test instruments. The chapter concludes with a discussion of the assessment environment including the most important criteria for authentic measurement, such as concept formation, open- endedness, forms of inquiry, sequential learning, and transferability.

Chapter 4 describes the training of the teachers and the process of assessing student portfolios, the study design, and methodologies. Topics discussed include Goals 2000, the national assessment standards, and state and local standards. Also discussed is the construction of the assessment instruments, authentic assessment, the specification of performances, and the design and use of the scoring rubrics. Details are provided on how portfolios are scored, how the teachers are trained to achieve scorespread, interjudge reliability, and handle discrepancies, and how to develop art curriculum.

Chapter 5 describes the activities of the Illinois project, which focused mostly on the development of electronic formats for portfolio design. Several examples of electronic portfolios developed by teachers and students are presented, including the Spring Brook and Forest Road elementary models, the Secondary Mundelein Model and the University Studies Model. Discussed are the objectives and benefits of each model, the standards used, the storage and handling of artwork, and the hard- and software that was employed.

Chapter 6 presents the conclusions and recommendations of the study including the results of the student portfolio assessment, the reliability of the measures, the quantification of expressive development, and the performance goals. Also included are suggestions for further study.

The appendixes include tables supporting studio portfolio assessment findings, a summary of the criteria art teachers use to evaluate student work and student performance, a summary of the criteria art students use to evaluate artwork at school and at home, and the criteria artists use to evaluate their work.

THE ASSESSMENT CONTEXT

The National Assessment Context

Over the past two decades, education in the United States has undergone phenomenal change. Fueled by both internal and external forces, challenges arose to previously held paradigms. Political, economic, social, cultural, and technological concerns all combined to drive the changes. Waves of educational reform precipitated by publication of *A Nation at Risk* (National Commission on Excellence in Education, 1983) and *Toward Civilization* (National Endowment for the Arts, 1988) continue today. By focusing national attention on the scope of public education, these two reports stimulated intense examination of its nature and quality.

Impact of the Standards Movement on Assessment

Much of the national educational reform effort focused on creation of standards. This standards movement rose from the realization that educators and other stakeholders showed only minimal agreement about numerous issues central to the education of students, including content, knowledge, skills, and processes. The content of disciplines was the source of much disagreement. In the field of art education, content was largely idiosyncratic and lacked uniformity. Numerous factors accounted for the divergence: differences in local resources, needs and values of the community, funding, facilities, and staffing. In addition, art education content frequently reflected art teachers' individual interest or skills and the quality of their pre-service training.

With the emergence of discipline-based art education in the mid-1980s and publication of the national fine arts standards (Music Educators National Conference, 1994), state departments of education and local school districts undertook ambitious visual arts curriculum initiatives. The goal was to provide consistent content and the result was restructured state visual arts proficiency guides and frameworks and local curriculum guides. In a study of state proficiency guides, Sabol (1994) found that their content reflected discipline-based art education content, which was compatible with the national visual arts standards.

Enter the National Assessment of Educational Progress

National concerns about improving the quality of education led to successive sets of federal goals from President Bush (U.S. Department of Education, 1991),

President Clinton (U.S. Department of Education, 1994), and the Congress (Improving America's School Act of 1994). The national education goals of 1994 included the visual arts. Even earlier, in 1969, Congress had mandated the National Assessment of Educational Progress (NAEP), whose purpose was to survey and monitor changes in the educational accomplishments of U.S. students. The NAEP has assessed learning in mathematics, reading, science, writing, world geography, U.S. history, civics, social studies, and the arts (Calderone, King, & Horkay, 1997).

The NAEP first assessed visual arts achievement in 1974 and 1978, raising numerous issues and concerns about the nature of assessment in art education (Sabol, 1990). The NAEP's findings prompted similar large-scale, state-level assessment in the 1980s (Sabol, 1990, 1994; Shuler & Connealy, 1998). The 1997 NAEP in visual arts consisted of items designed to measure eighth graders' knowledge and skills in creating and responding to art. The items were compatible with the national visual arts standards and with current classroom practices. Findings in The NAEP 1997 Arts Report Card (Persky, Sandene, & Askew, 1999) and ongoing secondary analysis of the 1997 NAEP visual arts data by researchers (Diket, Burton, & Sabol, 2000; Sabol, 2001a) again focused attention on national visual arts assessment, which in turn contributed to examinations of local assessment issues in visual arts education.

The Role of the Art Teacher in the Assessment Context

As schools and programs across the country implemented reforms in content standards, curriculum, and licensure standards, interest grew in measuring the reforms' effects on student achievements. The public's calls for accountability increased demands for evidence of student learning in all disciplines. People wanted to know whether national, state, and local standards were being met and to what degree. Visual arts education was no exception and over the past decade the focus on assessment has been felt in most art classrooms across the country. Numerous questions and concerns have arisen. For example, for what purposes do art teachers assess? When do they assess? What types of assessments do they use? What assessment training do art teachers have? What is assessment's impact on student work? What are teachers' attitudes and concerns about assessment in art education? What general effect has assessment had on art education?

These and numerous other questions required ongoing study, with art teachers a primary source of answers. Unfortunately, even as the national assessment movement and calls for accountability gathered strength, such fundamental questions received little attention and remain largely unanswered today. The essential role that art teachers play in designing, developing, selecting, conducting, interpreting, and reviewing assessments in their classrooms is critical to understanding the broad picture of assessment in art education. As the agents responsible for assessing student achievement, art teachers make myriad decisions affecting assessment. A variety of factors influences their decision-making processes; moreover, teachers' understanding of these factors often changes as they gain more assessment knowledge and experence.

Large-Scale Studies of Assessment in the Art Classroom

Several studies have identified how art teachers respond to assessment questions and issues. Sabol provided a range of findings from a broad sampling of art teachers: 1,000 urban art teachers (1998a), 1,000 rural art teachers (1999a), 1,000 new members from 16 states in the Western Region of the National Art Education Association (2001b), 500 art teachers from Indiana (1999b), and 600 art teachers from Pennsylvania (Sabol & Bensur, 2000). Findings from these studies will be compared to studies of 59 art teachers, 472 art students, and 50 artists who participated in Assessment Training Institutes (ATI) sponsored by the National Endowment for the Arts in 2000 and 2001 in Florida, Illinois, and Indiana. In-depth discussion of the Institutes will be provided in chapter 4.

Participants in each of the studies were randomly selected and included art teachers from the elementary, middle, and secondary instructional levels. Each study used questionnaires with closed-form, open-ended, and Likert-type attitude measurement items.   Parallel item content on questionnaires permitted cross-comparisons of findings from individual studies. Such comparisons produced a number of common findings for the studies' 4,159 art teachers. References to selected findings will be given to provide context and support for various issues and themes that follow.

Why Do Art Teachers Assess?

Assessment is conducted in art education for a variety of purposes that vary from school district to school district, from school to school, from program to programs, and from teacher to teacher. Frequently, assessment purposes and goals are not established for school districts or art programs. Although art teachers routinely engage in assessment in some form, whether formal or informal, they often do not have adequate understanding of the purposes of assessment or a well-considered list of their own purposes. As a result, assessment programs may be poorly structured, ill conceived, and uncoordinated. Without clearly identified assessment purposes, accurate measurements of student achievement are suspect. Results may not be completely understood and the full range of their meaning may not have been considered. Results may be meaningless or irrelevant to the districts' and programs' educational goals and unrelated to the students' comprehensive art education. To create appropriate assessment programs, art teachers and other educators must clearly identify purposes—whatever they may be—and understand how to achieve them.

Studies conducted during the Assessment Training Institutes and others (Sabol, 1999a, 1999b; Sabol & Bensur, 2000) in which art teachers were asked to identify purposes of their assessments revealed that many were held in common. Some were established by school districts and were required for art programs, whereas others were created by art teachers for their individual schools or programs. Listed in their order of priority, purposes of assessments included the following: to grade student achievement, to provide student feedback, to provide instructional feedback to students, to evaluate art education curriculum, to set student art education goals and standards, to diagnose student art education needs, to set art education program goals and standards, to evaluate teaching, and to identify strengths and weaknesses of the art education program. A limited number of additional purposes were reported by art teachers and were given significantly lower priority.

Examination of identified purposes suggests that the most common focused on students and their needs. Of lesser importance were assessments of curriculum, programs, and teaching. Whereas student-related assessment purposes are rightly of most immediate concern in the educational scheme of things, the curriculum, programs, and teaching are directly linked to student achievement. In the long term, greater emphasis on conducting additional assessment in these areas or examining assessment results with these perspectives in mind may have more far-reaching power to positively affect student achievement in the art classroom.

What Types of Assessments Do Art Teachers Use?

Each assessment measure has distinct advantages, disadvantages, and limitations. Knowledge of these distinctions is essential for art teachers to successfully select appropriate measures: those that will provide evidence of student achievement while being compatible with the art program's goals and assessment purposes.

Most assessment measures can be grouped into standardized, alternative, or authentic categories (Sabol & Zimmerman, 1997). Each category's qualities make it unique. Standardized measures required common procedures, apparatus, and scoring criteria so that precisely the same test can be given at different times and places (Cronbach, 1960, p. 22). In some assessment situations, standardized tests are the preferred method because they impose uniform testing conditions through controls such as standardized directions and time limits. In addition, they permit uniform evaluations of students and permit comparisons of scores with those from other groups or with established standards of performance. Summaries of pooled scores from large populations provide a range of performances called norms. Established norms enable teachers to determine the relative performance of an individual or group to that of a much larger group.

Standardized tests must meet requirements for validity and reliability. Validity is determined by the degree to which a total test and its individual items match the universe of knowledge or course content (Cronbach, 1960). Beattie (1997) identified 12 criteria for establishing validity of performance-based assessments: relevance, content fidelity and integrity, exhaustiveness, cognitive complexity, equity, meaningfulness, straightforwardness, cohesiveness, consequences, directness, cost and efficiency, and generalizability. Reliability is the extent to which test scores are consistent, dependable, and repeatable (Cronbach, 1960). To provide reliable results, standardized tests must provide accurate results over a period of time and under a variety of conditions. The defining qualities of standardized tests mean that few are available for measuring visual arts achievement and those that exist may not be usable in many of the settings or instructional levels at which art education is conducted.

Alternative assessments provide another avenue for gathering evidence of student achievement in visual arts education. Sabol and Zimmerman (1997) defined alternative assessment as nontraditional and different from standardized measures in the past. Chittendon (1991) stated that alternative assessment is teacher mediated and theory referenced, in contrast to standardized assessments that are externally designed and norm referenced. Typically, alternative assessments do not include traditional paper-and-pencil item formats. However, these demonstrations may not mimic knowledge, skills, and processes used by professionals within a discipline, for example, by artists, art historians, aestheticians, and art critics. Alternative assessments may include measures such as games, puzzles, worksheets, checklists, and the like.

Authentic assessments differ from standardized and alternative measures in that they are performance based and include real-life decisions and behaviors of professionals in a discipline. Armstrong (1994) characterized authentic assessments as legitimate in that they are intellectually challenging but responsive to the student and the school. Authentic assessment does not focus on factual knowledge as an end in itself. Rather, it focuses on the ability to use relevant knowledge, skills, and processes for solving open-ended problems during meaningful tasks. Another key factor that distinguishes authentic assessments from traditional ones is that they provide opportunities for students to integrate many kinds of learning.

Whether formative, summative, standardized, authentic, alternative, or created by a teacher or an assessment specialist, no assessment measure can capture all types and levels of learning that occur in the art classroom. Indeed, if every possible type of measure was used on every student product, significant learning would remain unmeasured because the highly complex nature of learning that routinely occurs in the art classroom.

Art teachers use a wide variety of assessments. Sabol conducted a study of the variety of assessments art teachers in the Assessment Training Institutes used.

From this study and others by Sabol (1998a, 1999a, 1999b, 2001a) and Sabol and Bensur (2000) the most common types were identified. Listed in order of priority, they include: work samples, professional judgment, teacher-developed tests, portfolios, discussions, critiques, sketchbooks, checklists, exhibits, reports, and research papers. Other assessments used less frequently included journals, questionnaires, anecdotal records, interviews, puzzles and games, standardized tests, video recordings and audio recordings.

Among all the groups surveyed, only modest differences exist for the types of assessments used. The types selected by art teachers varied slightly by instructional levels. Elementary teachers used the fewest types of measures and secondary art teachers the most. New art teachers used fewer types than did more experienced art teachers (Sabol, 2001a). Assessments that involve writing, such as reports, research papers, and journals, were used more frequently at the secondary level than at other instructional levels. Nearly twice as many secondary art teachers used critiques compared to the percentage using critiques at other instructional levels.

What Assessment Training Have Art Teachers Had?

Recent scrutiny of educational achievement and public calls for accountability have caused assessment to become an essential component of contemporary art education. Art teachers must now become experts in another field of knowledge, one easily as complex as curriculum theory, curriculum development models, discipline content, and instructional methodology. They must have in-depth knowledge of assessment's terminology, methods, and processes. They must be able to interpret assessment data and to communicate their meaning to students, colleagues, administrators, school boards, and other stakeholders. Moreover, as the field of assessment continues to expand, and as questions and issues about its use in art education arise, art teachers must keep their knowledge current. Preservice education about assessment, as well as ongoing professional development, is essential. How do teachers today acquire their assessment knowledge and skills? Where do they receive training and gain experience in applying it?

Findings from studies by Sabol during the Assessment Training Institutes and by Sabol (1999b) and Sabol and Bensur (2000) identified sources for art teachers' assessment training. Findings were comparable across all instructional levels. Less than one half of art teachers reported that they received assessment training from college courses. Slightly over 40% received some training in undergraduate courses. One third received training at workshops or conferences. Approximately one fourth reported that they were self-taught and gained assessment knowledge through trial and error or on-the-job experience. Less than a fifth of art teachers received assessment training at in-service sessions sponsored by the local school district. Disturbing findings from these studies reveal that approximately one fourth (23.9%) of art teachers reported no assessment training. Others reported that they gained assessment information from colleagues, professional journals or magazines. These studies suggest that, as a group, art teachers lack fundamental knowledge, skills, and training in assessment. Clearly, the recent increased emphasis placed on assessment in art education requires an equally increased effort in providing necessary assessment education for art teachers.

What Attitudes Do Art Teachers Hold About Assessment?

Attitudes are an immensely important component in the human psyche. They strongly influence all of our decisions. They greatly affect actions we take toward objects. For example, to a large extent we choose the things we do because we like them. They affect evaluations of events and objects. We make judgments, in part, based on how something meets our needs or confirms preexisting attitudes. We also perceive problems based on our attitudes and design solutions compatible with our attitudes. Knowledge of attitudes and their influence on people provides a unique perspective for understanding teachers' issues and questions about assessment.

Louis Thurstone is the social psychologist credited with developing and popularizing measurement of attitudes. Attitude scales he developed in the 1930s and 1940s are standard instruments still in use today. In 1928 he defined attitude as "the sum total of a man's inclinations and feelings, prejudice and bias, preconceived notions, ideas, fears, threats, and convictions about any specified topic" (p. 531). Later he simplified his definition by saying, "Attitude is the affect for or against a psychological object" (1931, p. 261). Mueller defined attitude as "(1) affect for or against, (2) evaluation of, (3) like or dislike of, or (4) positiveness or negativeness toward a psychological object" (1986, p. 3).

Value is an important construct in understanding attitudes. A highly abstract construct, value lacks definitional consensus. As a result it is harder to conceptualize clearly. Mueller stated that:

> Like attitudes, values involve evaluating. But it is generally agreed among social theorists that values are more abstract, higher-order constructs than attitudes. They are thus more permanent and resistant to change, and they have a direct or indirect causal influence on both attitudes and behaviors. There is general agreement that values cause attitudes. More specifically, an attitude toward an object is a function of the extent to which that object is perceived to facilitate the attainment of important values. (1986, p. 5)

He emphasized that:

> Values are determinants of attitudes. Let us be clear, though, that there is not a one-to-one relationship between particular attitudes and particular values. Rather, a single attitude is "caused" by many values—by one's whole value system, in fact. (p. 5)

Attitudes of art teachers toward assessment are a significant component of the educational context. Examinations of these attitudes provide understanding of the teachers' actions and the underlying values that influence them. Because art teachers have primary responsibility for conducting assessments and interpreting the results, and because they directly influence what students learn and what students create, study of art teachers' attitudes toward assessment provides a clearer picture of assessment's effects in the overall scheme of art education and of the values art education embraces and promotes.

Sabol, during the Assessment Training Institutes, Sabol (1999b), and Sabol and Bensur (2000) studied attitudes of art teachers toward a number of issues related to assessment. Attitude measurement instruments developed for these studies included Likert-type items. Likert-type scales locate a respondent's attitude toward something on an affective continuum ranging from "very positive" to "very negative."

Attitudes about Purposes of Assessment

Purposes for assessment in art education vary from school to school. Art teacher attitudes toward purposes of assessment influence their decisions in selecting instruments and in acting to meet the purposes. In two studies (Sabol, 1999b; Sabol & Bensur, 2000), art teachers were asked if they shared assessment results with administrators. Over half of art teachers agreed that they did, whereas one fourth did not. Attitudes about whether parents expected assessment in art education programs were comparable. Half of art teachers studied agreed that parents expected assessment. A belief in using assessments for instructional purposes was among the most common attitudes held. Over two thirds of art teachers agreed that assessment should be used for this purpose. Art teachers even more strongly agreed that assessments are useful to evaluate their teaching and their programs.

Attitudes about Implementing Assessments

Engaging in assessment programs and conducting assessments involves another cluster of attitudes. Art teachers must determine which assessment methods will meet identified purposes and then implement them. A common assessment instrument is paper-and-pencil tests. Art teachers' attitudes about these tests' effectiveness were clear. They strongly believed (84%) that paper-and-pencil tests were not the best method for assessing what students have learned. However, art teachers (58%) agreed that portfolios were the best way to evaluate what students had learned in art.

The studies also explored attitudes toward the time needed before, during, or after classes to conduct assessments. Art teachers disagree that assessment of student learning was too time consuming. Only 20% thought it was too time consuming. Most teachers agreed (54%) that they had enough time to assess students regularly. However, 34% felt they did not have enough time—a higher percentage than the 20% who saw assessment as too time consuming. These findings suggest that, although as a group art teachers feel they have enough time to assess students and that assessment is not too time consuming, a significant number see the activity as too time consuming and difficult to do regularly.

Attitudes about Assessment Training

Art teachers require a base of knowledge from which to build assessment programs and the field of assessment is growing in content, including basic vocabulary, measures, strategies, administration procedures, research methodologies, and applications. In order to remain current with such growth, art teachers must receive training. Some receive preservice preparation for assessment, whereas others receive training on an ongoing basis throughout their teaching careers. Because of these differences and as for any knowledge base, teachers possess varying degrees of understanding and skill in assessment.

When asked if they knew how to evaluate students' learning in art, the teachers strongly held the attitude that they did (85%); however, fewer (51%) felt they had sufficient knowledge about assessment methods. Art teachers were asked if they had had assessment training in courses, workshops, or in-service sessions. Nearly two thirds responded that they had, and a third said they had not. Thus, although many art teachers have had some assessment training and most strongly feel they know how to assess students' work, they feel less strongly that they know enough about methods to do it. Some art teachers reported that their assessment training focused on theory and philosophical issues and did not provide practical or hands-on experience usable in their classrooms. Some reported receiving training in assessment of mathematics learning, multiple intelligences assessment, attitude assessment, and other assessment-related topics that may not be meaningful for measuring visual arts achievement. In art teachers' assessment training greater emphasis needs to be placed on direct application to the art classroom and a broader array of methods that focus on art learning.

General Attitudes about Assessment in Art Education

Overarching attitudes about fundamental philosophical issues influence attitudes about related or lesser concerns. The teachers' attitudes discussed thus far are, in part, extensions of their beliefs about larger underlying questions.

Of significant importance is the fundamental question of whether student artwork should be assessed. Lowenfeldian philosophy holds that children's artwork should not be assessed. By contrast, the discipline-based approach to art education advocates assessment. Knowing which philosophical stance art teachers embrace is of importance in fully understanding their attitudes about specific assessment issues. Additionally, one must keep in mind the goals that local school districts adopt for art education and the differences in those goals from the standpoints of developmental and instructional levels. Elementary and secondary art teachers' goals may differ. How teachers view themselves as agents responsible for achieving those goals and how those views are compatible with their overall philosophical stances is central to interpreting their attitudes about assessment.

When asked if student artwork should be assessed, art teachers strongly agreed (82%) that it should. Although philosophical perspectives were not identified for art teachers, these findings suggest that Lowenfeldian or discipline-based art education approaches were not factors influencing this attitude. The strong belief in assessment was held across instructional levels: 80% of elementary art teachers and 83% of secondary art teachers.

In a related question, art teachers were asked to express their attitudes about whether art education includes types of learning that cannot be assessed. Attitudes were more widely distributed on this question. Nearly three fifths agreed that there are types of learning in art that cannot be assessed; however, the remaining two fifths disagreed or were undecided about this issue.

A fundamental component of the visual arts is personal expression and by its very nature personal expression suggests the absence of generalizable standards from which it can be judged. Personal expression is a principal component that contributes to the unique scope and content of art education. When asked if they felt that personal expression could be assessed, nearly three fourths of art teachers thought it could. Viewing the efficacy of assessment in its broadest perspective, the art teachers were asked to describe their attitudes. Half of the teachers felt assessment has had a positive effect on art education. Nearly a fifth of those thought it was important for informing students, parents, administrators, and the community about student achievement in visual arts education. Another fifth felt assessment provided credibility for art education programming, whereas others felt it was important for measuring student achievement and for determining the effectiveness of teaching and to evaluate the effectiveness of their curriculum. More than a quarter of the art teachers felt assessment was a necessary evil and an additional sixth felt it had a negative impact on art education. Art teachers were asked if they strongly supported assessment in art education. Overwhelmingly (86%), they strongly supported it.

Negative and Positive Effects of Assessment In Art Education

The findings about general attitudes toward assessment suggest that art teachers are aware of assessment's negative and positive effects in art education. Open-ended items provided opportunities for the teachers to express more fully their views about these effects. When asked to describe drawbacks related to assessment, they reported a wide array of them. The most common drawbacks, listed in order of priority, were:
1. Too many students and not enough time to assess.
2. Lack of uniform performance standards, guidelines, procedures, inefficient assessment tools.
3. Changes the focus of art education from art learning to assessment results.
4. Involves too much subjectivity.
5. Inability of assessments to measure a broad range of learning.
6. Increased student anxiety, lowered self-esteem, emotional upsets.
7. Inability to accurately and precisely assess personal expression.
8. Stifling of creativity, restrictive.
9. Increased teacher anxiety.
10. Lack of assessment knowledge and training.
11. Assessments drive curriculum.
12. Takes away studio time.
Responses were similar across instructional levels. Surprisingly, nearly one tenth of the teachers reported that they felt assessment had no negative impact on their program or the field of art education.

In describing positive effects of assessment, once again, a wide array of effects was reported. The most common positive effects, listed in order of priority, were that assessment:
1. Makes students more aware of goals for the program and more accountable.
2. Provides feedback for students and teachers about learning, shows growth.
3. Helps students better understand assignments, improves work.
4. Improves student motivation, provides accountability for students.
5. Provides credibility for the art education program.

6. Indicates whether goals and objectives of the program are being met.

7. Improves student self-esteem.

8. Improves teaching and makes teachers more introspective.

9. Improves students' understanding of their grades.

10. Makes parents aware of the program's goals.

11. Increases respect from administrators.

12. Motivates students to work harder.

Responses were similar across instructional levels. A small percentage of the teachers 8% reported that they felt assessment has had no positive impact on art education.

This summary of findings of studies about the relationship of assessment to art education suggests that art teachers possess a generally acceptable level of understanding about assessment, are aware of its importance in art education, and embrace it in their programs. Yet, the findings also reveal that art teachers are keenly aware of, and understand, the numerous drawbacks assessment brings to art education. Additionally, the findings identified art teachers' deficiencies in assessment knowledge and areas in need of further professional development.

The Art Classroom Assessment Context

Assessment, in the broadest sense, involves identification of goals and purposes, selection of procedures, methods, and measures, coordination of timing, analysis of data, interpretation of results, and formulation of responses to the results. Of primary importance in any assessment is selection of criteria on which to base the assessments. Criteria represent the standards to which performances and artifacts will be judged. They create the central focus of the assessment and provide boundaries or limitations for the assessment. Ultimately, they represent the central or most important characteristics of the performances or artifacts the assessment will review and evaluate.

Art teachers assess a wide variety of learning and artifacts within their programs. With the dominance of discipline-based art education over the past decade, many art teachers have become concerned with assessing evidence of learning in aesthetics, art history, and art criticism, in addition to assessing studio production. However, not all art teachers have embraced the discipline-based art education model and some who have do not routinely include learning experiences in aesthetics, art criticism, and art history. Without question, a historic tradition of art education programming has been to maintain a principal and dominant focus on studio production. Studio production provides experiences designed to focus on the core of what is taught and learned in art education programs and provides the frame of reference for learning in aesthetics, art criticism, and art history. Learning in these areas could not take place without references to studio products. As a result, assessing studio products is a pivotal activity necessary for determining what and the extent to which students are learning in art classrooms.

Selecting Criteria for Evaluating Works of Art

Works of art are subjected to evaluation by almost anyone who comes in contact with them. In fact, models for conducting evaluations and arriving at judgments about works of art have been developed and are taught in most schools. Whether they employ these models or not, people use a variety of criteria when conducting their evaluations. Criteria may be well considered and carefully chosen or they may be ill considered and randomly adopted. They may change with each work of art or over time. Experience, knowledge of art, and personal preferences influence the selection of criteria. Selections may be the result of conscious thought or intuition.

One factor that influences the selection process is the purpose of the evaluation. As purposes of the evaluations change, so may the criteria selections change. In the case of the casual consumer of works of art, criteria may be chosen for different purposes from those of an art teacher, a student of art, or an artist. It is likely that there will be some degree of agreement among criteria chosen by people from each of these groups; however, it is equally likely that there will be distinct differences in chosen criteria due to differing purposes. A degree of consensus exists among art teachers about the purposes for which evaluation of student artwork should be done. Those purposes were previously discussed. Aside from the question of what common purposes for assessment exist among art teachers and how those purposes influence the selection of criteria, many other related questions emerge. For example, what criteria do those who make art, including students and artists, use to evaluate their work? How do they arrive at decisions to select them? Are those criteria similar to or different from those used by art teachers and consumers of art? Do criteria selections change over time?

What Factors Contribute to such Changes and Why?

Studies that identify criteria art teachers use to evaluate student artwork or that identify criteria artists and students of art use to evaluate their work and the work of others have not been conducted previously. Answers to these questions have the potential to influence art education in the areas of curriculum, instruction, and the assessment of works of art.

Examining Criteria Used to Evaluate Works of Art

To determine what criteria art teachers, students of art, and artists use to evaluate works of art, three studies were done as part of the Assessment Institute Training (AIT) project. Participants in these studies included 59 elementary-, middle-, and secondary-level art teachers, 472 of their students, and 50 artists. Separate questionnaires for the three groups were developed. Questions were designed to determine what criteria art teachers, art students, and artists use to evaluate their work and that of others. Parallel content in selected items permitted cross-comparisons of responses among the three groups. Answers on the questionnaires were compared to identify similarities and differences among the groups.

A Study of Art Teachers in the ATI Project and Assessment

The art teachers who participated in the AIT project were asked to participate in a study of questions related to assessment in their programs. The study was designed to provide insight into art teachers' views and attitudes and about issues related to the research questions. The study was designed to investigate demographic profiles of art teachers participating in the institutes, curriculum sources, instructional methods, purposes of assessment, frequencies of assessment, types of assessments used, previous assessment training, effects of assessment on student work, evaluation criteria selection methods, methods of communicating evaluation criteria to students, criteria selected to evaluate student work, changes in selected evaluation criteria over time, and attitudes about assessment. To understand the nature of criteria art teachers use in the art classroom context, selected references are made to findings from this study.

How Art Teachers Select Evaluation Criteria for Studio Work

Art teachers consider a variety of issues when selecting criteria from which to evaluate students' studio products. The most commonly reported reasons were how well the criteria matched the objectives of the lesson and how well the criteria matched the content or concepts taught in the lesson. Art teachers chose evaluation criteria second most frequently, based on how well they matched the local curriculum guide content, state proficiency guide content, or national visual arts standards. Criteria also were selected by the characteristics observed in students' work, by the needs of the students, by trial and error, by how well they matched the intent of the work with the product, by the level of art teachers' knowledge of assessment, by how well they matched state-level assessments, and by how well they measured students' growth.

Criteria Art Teachers Use to Evaluate Students' Artwork

Evaluations of students' artwork, whether they are represented in the form of grades, written or oral reports, or some other manner, are the product of an assessment process that involves application of a set of criteria to arrive at a judgment about the work. The set of criteria may change from project to project, class to class, course to course, and so on. The set may be formally documented and exist as a specified list or may be informal and exist as a generalizable framework. Criteria may be communicated to students through several methods and may be used at various times during the creative process. These considerations contribute to the procedures used to select criteria and to their application. However, at the core of the evaluation process is a bank or "menu of criteria" from which art teachers may choose. As a set, evaluation criteria represent standards or characteristics by which art teachers measure quality in their students' artwork. Art teachers focus their instruction on content and activities that are delimited by the constructs represented in the criteria set. In considering the issue of criteria sets, the question of whether art teachers have consensus about criteria in such a set arises.

Agreement about curriculum content for the field of art education is found in the National Visual Arts Standards (Music Educators National Conference, 1994) and in state visual arts proficiency guides (Sabol, 1994). Other studies designed to identify common content of state achievement tests (Sabol, 1994, 1998a), commonly used assessment methods, purposes of assessment, assessment training of art teachers (Sabol, 1998b, 1999a, 1999b, 2001a; Sabol & Bensur, 2000), and common attitudes of art teachers toward assessment (Sabol, 1998b, 1999a, 1999b, 2001a; Sabol & Bensur, 2000) have produced findings about levels of agreement among art teachers related to these concerns. However, studies designed to identify commonly agreed-upon criteria used by art teachers to evaluate their students' artwork are lacking.

Art teachers in the ATI project were asked to identify the range of assessment criteria they use to evaluate their students' studio products. A set of 23 criteria resulted (see Appendix A). High levels of agreement were produced for each of the identified criteria. Nearly total agreement was produced for five criteria studied. Among these criteria, the elements of art, the principles of design, composition or use of space, and creativity (94.9% each) were identified. These were followed by following directions, technical skill or craftsmanship, work meeting assignment objectives, personal expression, completing processes correctly, attention to detail and originality, and improvement or growth. Two thirds or more of art teachers reported that they used representation of space or distance, knowledge of concepts, work matching intent, experimentation or risk taking, and sophistication of theme or idea to evaluate students' studio products. Other criteria were used less frequently.

Criteria Art Teachers Use to Evaluate Students' Performance

Evaluation of students' achievement in art programs is generally not the sole result of the evaluation of the studio products they create. Student performance in the art classroom consists of additional indicators of students' actions and learning. These indicators may be unrelated to the content or skills in the discipline. They may have no direct connection to students' artistic ability or the products they create. Student behaviors and other considerations related to personal traits may be included in this group. They are, nonetheless, important for measuring the comprehensive performance of students in art programs. When evaluations from these criteria are combined with evaluations of students' studio products, clearer assessment of student achievement results.

High levels of agreement about the set of criteria used to evaluate students' performance were found among art teachers. Of the 18 criteria listed, 13 were used by half or more of the art teachers to evaluate students' performances (see Appendix B). Three fourths of art teachers or more responded that effort, problem-solving ability, improvement or growth, classroom behavior, and self-motivation or initiative were commonly used to evaluate students' performance in their art programs. Half or more of art teachers identified turning the assignments in on time and using previous knowledge, reflection, thoughtfulness or metacognition, critical thinking and decision making, synthesis of ideas, following clean-up procedures, and problem identification as criteria they used to evaluate performances. Other criteria were used significantly less by art teachers. The most common criterion, "effort", was used for student evaluation at the elementary level more widely than at the middle or secondary levels. Classroom behavior, self-motivation and initiative, turning assignments in on time, and use of previous knowledge were more commonly reported by middle and secondary art teachers than those at the elementary level.

How Criteria Used to Evaluate Student Artwork Changed Over Time

The set of criteria art teachers use to evaluate students' studio products changes over time. Change may be the result of newly gained knowledge or training. Thinking in the field of assessment is continuously evolving. Change may be imposed by decision makers or the wishes of the public. Demands for demonstrations of accountability continue to be made as a means of proving to the public that learning is occurring in schools. Developments within the field of art education contribute to its changes. New content standards or curriculum revisions contribute to changes in assessment. New purposes or goals of the art education program contribute to change. Art teachers frequently are unaware of the nature of some changes. They may be unaware of the effects changes may have on their programs and the work of their students. Inevitably, whatever the source or impetus for change, art teachers make decisions about how to implement change in their programs. Art teachers alter criteria selections for evaluating students' studio products to keep pace with these changes.

Art teachers in the ATI project were asked to reflect on changes they made in selecting evaluation criteria over time and to describe the nature of these changes. They responded that evaluation criteria generally were becoming more focused on the "process" of making art and the thinking that accompanied it, rather than on the final "product" that resulted from the process. In this regard, processes included not only the physical and cognitive processes related to manipulating media, but also the cognitive processes involved in problem identification, creative thinking, critical thinking, problem solving, synthesis of knowledge, evaluation, and so on. Purposes such as providing students instructional feedback, setting goals for students, and diagnosing students' strengths and weaknesses lend themselves to increased focus on the processes of making art and on the product. Further evidence supporting increased emphasis on process is found in the types of assessments art teachers frequently use to evaluate their students' studio work. Work samples, critiques, discussions, journals, questionnaires, and interviews were commonly used. These measures focus considerably on processes involved in making art and on final products.

Descriptions of how the set of evaluation criteria used by art teachers to evaluate students' studio products has changed were grouped into the following categories:

1. Increasingly focused on the "process" of making art.
2. Were more detailed and specific.
3. Were more comprehensive and expanded
4. Reflected the art teacher's increased knowledge about assessment and were more sophisticated.
6. Focused more on writing.
7. Changed with the needs of students and classes.
8. Haven't changed.
9. Focused more on a broader spectrum of learning that goes on in the class room.
10. Included student input.
11. Were more simplified.
12. Were more objective.
13. Focused more on the performance of the class than on individual students.
14. Reflected the impact of discipline-based art education.

Most art teachers reported more than one type of change. Significant differences were not common among instructional levels, with the exceptions of "more emphasis on writing" and "included student input," which were primarily identified by secondary art teachers, and "focused more on the performance of the class than on individual students" and "reflected the impact of discipline-based art education," which were reported by elementary art teachers alone.

Asking Students About Assessment in Art Education

Students are central characters in the assessment-in-art-education milieu. They play an important role in fully understanding the overall impact of assessment on art education. As participants in the assessment process, they are in the unique position of experiencing the assessment process first hand. All too often, students are not included in the exploration of issues that concern them. They are not consulted and they are not given opportunities to express their views. Examination of their perspective provides an additional opportunity to better understand the impact of assessment on art education. Students of art teachers in the ATI project from Florida and Indiana were asked to complete a brief questionnaire containing items about their assessment experiences. A total of 472 students, including 185 elementary, 110 middle school, and 171 secondary students participated in the study. A discussion of selected views of these students follows.

Criteria Students Use to Evaluate Artwork at School

Students in art classes continuously engage in evaluation of artwork they make. Evaluations may be focused or directed by criteria provided by the teacher. In this case, students' decisions may be structured or manipulated in order to meet the objectives of the activity or to focus work of the activities. Often students will expand teacher-provided criteria to include additional considerations of importance to them.

Students were asked to identify criteria they used to evaluate studio products made at school (see Appendix C). Most commonly used criteria included use of the elements of art, skill with art materials, following directions, details in the work, neatness, representation of ideas, experimentation, use of space, learning something new, and new or different ideas. Other listed criteria were less commonly selected. Additional criteria independently identified by students included "if my friends like it," "if it is 'cool,'" "if it matched the teachers' example," "if it looked better than the work of other students in the class," and other criteria with no apparent relationship to works of art.

Analysis of preferred criteria based on the instructional level of students revealed distinct differences. Listed in order of priority, elementary students used the following criteria most frequently: use of the elements of art, skill, following the art teachers' directions, details in the work, and neatness. Middle school students preferred the following criteria: use of the elements of art, skill, following the art teachers' directions, details in the work, and neatness. Secondary art students mostly used the following prioritized list of criteria: use of the elements of art, skill, following the art teachers' directions, details in the work, and neatness. The percentage of students reporting use of each criterion decreased at each instructional level. This finding suggests that elementary art students used these criteria more frequently than students at other levels; however, analysis of secondary and middle school students' responses for other criteria revealed that they use a broader variety of criteria or place greater value on other criteria in evaluating their studio work than elementary students. For example, secondary (48%) and middle school students' (41%) selection of the criterion "use of the principles of design" was more frequent than elementary students' (38%). Other similar examples of instructional level differences in criteria selection by students were identified.

Students' Art Making at Home

Students often make art at home. Students of art teachers in the project made art in classes at school. Making art in those classes was a requirement and art activities and other aspects of the activity were largely selected and managed by the art teachers. At home, students have freedom to make such selections. Choices normally made by the art teacher become the providence of the student. Decisions about the media or materials with which to work, the theme or message of the work, the amount of time the student will spend making the work, when to work, and numerous other issues are made by the student. Students choose to make art at home for reasons known to them alone. These reasons may be the same as or different from those identified for making art at school.

Students were asked if they made art at home. A total of 379 (80%) responded that they did. The largest group of students who made artwork at home was elementary students followed by secondary students and middle school students. These students were asked to identify reasons they made art at home. The most commonly identified reason was that "it is fun." This reason was followed by "It helps me relax," "It helps me express my ideas," "To pass my time," and "It is my hobby." Students most frequently responding that they made art at home because "it is fun" were secondary students (84%), followed by elementary students (82%) and middle school students (78%). Secondary art students (72%) most frequently responded that they made art at home to relax, followed by middle (61%) and elementary students (60%).

Both elementary and secondary students responded most frequently that they made art at home to express their ideas (56% each), whereas middle school students (45%) responded less frequently.

Criteria Students Use to Evaluate Artwork Made at Home

The purposes for which students make art at home contribute to selecting criteria by which to evaluate their work. Evaluation of artwork made at home, as opposed to artwork made at school, may not be formally done by students. Some purposes, such as making it for fun, may require evaluations that do not focus on the quality of the artwork, but rather on the experience of making it. Involvement in the process of making becomes the purpose of the work. Evaluation of it consists of determining the degree of enjoyment the student received; other criteria that are linked to the work of art may be overlooked or disregarded entirely. This is not to say that criteria and evaluation processes taught and learned in school, which may be internalized, are not used at home. Instead, it suggests that the point of the evaluation may shift to become more personal. In this sense, evaluation may not be related to a set of concise standards of performance or predetermined goals for the product, but, rather, it may be measured by more subjective scales and criteria.

Students were asked to identify evaluation criteria they frequently used to evaluate artwork they made at home (see Appendix D). They identified skill with media most frequently. This criterion was followed by "how much it pleased me," neatness, use of the elements of art, details, how well space was filled, and the degree of experimentation or uniqueness. Other criteria were used less frequently.

Comparisons of responses among instructional levels of students and criteria revealed distinctive differences. At the elementary level, students ranked use of the elements first, followed by skill with art materials and details in work, neatness, and "It pleased me." Middle school students ranked use of the elements of art first, followed by details, neatness, "It pleased me," and skill with art materials. Secondary students ranked use of the elements of art and "It pleased me" first, followed by skill with materials, details, and neatness. Secondary students as a group used a wider array of criteria from which to evaluate their work than middle school and elementary students. By contrast, elementary students used fewer criteria, but higher percentages of elementary students used the smaller set of selected criteria than those from other instructional levels.

Looking at Artists and Assessment

Artists are engaged continuously with assessment of their work. Assessment may be focused on individual works of their art or upon the body of their work. Reasons for assessing their work may change over the course of their careers, as may the criteria selected for evaluating it. Artists' evaluations do not always focus on their own work. They may extend to evaluations of works of art from the past as found in the history of art or to the works artists are creating currently. A number of questions about assessment and its connections with artists arise. For example, for what purposes do artists evaluate their works of art? What criteria do artists use in these evaluations? How have these criteria changed over time? Do artists use similar criteria to evaluate their work and that of other artists? These and other related questions may provide unique perspectives that art teachers and students of art should consider. Artists' answers to these questions may help expand or confirm assessment practices and criteria choices used to evaluate works of art made in art classes and at home. Potentially, they may reveal ways in which assessment can be made more meaningful and useful for art teachers and their students.

To explore answers to the previous questions, a study of 50 randomly selected artists from Florida and Indiana was done as part of the AIT project. Lists of artists were provided by the Indiana Arts Commission, Very Special Arts Indiana, the Florida Division of Cultural Affairs, participating art teachers, and institute directors. A questionnaire including items about demographics and evaluation criteria was sent to them.

Criteria Artists Use to Evaluate Their Work

Previously, the criteria art teachers and students of art use to evaluate art were discussed. Those discussions included examinations of influences on the selection of sets of criteria for those groups. Artists are subject to many of the same influences as art teachers and their students in making their selections. For art teachers and students, outcomes associated with the end results of evaluations may be found in degrees of personal satisfaction, productive use of free time, grades, student records, access to special programming, and, perhaps, admissions to colleges and universities. The purposes for evaluation are primarily academic or leisure related. By contrast, for artists, the purposes of evaluation and the outcomes they produce have a different emphasis. Outcomes of evaluations by artists of their work can change the courses of their careers, their financial status, their social standing, and, perhaps, their place in the history of art. The importance of the outcomes of evaluations for artists are more long ranged in their effect and the consequences are seemingly more acute. This is not to say that the evaluation process used by artists dictates the course of their livelihood or standing, nor does it say that evaluations of student artwork are of less value and importance. However, it does represent an aspect of making art that requires artists to be more introspective and reflective about the meaning of evaluations and the actions they take as a result of them.

Artists were asked to identify criteria they used to evaluate their work (see Appendix E). "Originality" was the most frequently selected criterion. It was followed in order of priority by: improvement or growth; composition; development of personal style, expression, or aesthetic; technical skill with media; development or expansion of previously used ideas; successful communication of ideas; effective use of the principles of design; and effective use of the elements of art. Other criteria were selected less frequently.

Criteria Artists Use to Evaluate Other Artists' Work

Criteria artists use to evaluate their own work have a personal meaning and connection to the artists. They represent the things artists believe are most important in their work. They represent what artists are trying to accomplish in and through their work. These criteria are subjective and go through changes as the artist sees fit to alter them, but do artists use the same criteria to evaluate the work of fellow artists? If not, how are the criteria they use different?

Artists said they used the same criteria to evaluate their work and the work of other artists. Several wrote that, even though the criteria may be the same, the standards of quality for an individual criterion may be lower when judging work of other artists. Several artists wrote that their criteria were more "understanding" or more "accepting" when applied to the work of others.

Some artists offered an additional list of criteria for evaluating the work of other artists. The prioritized list of those criteria includes the following: originality, "Does it come alive for me?" or "Does it speak to me?," technical skill, "Context of the work," effective expression of ideas, style, triteness, "Is the idea overused?," "Does the work have truth?," "Does it create a visual impact?," "How does it compare to my cultural experience?," "Does it show intensity of labor?," composition, effective use of the elements of art, "Does the work match the artists' intent," "Does the work have beauty?," "How does it affect the senses?," and "Does it inspire me?"

A number of the criteria included on this list also were included in the set of criteria artists use to evaluate their work. Further study is needed to determine why criteria included on this list are not included on the list of criteria used by artists in evaluating their own work.

Comparing Criteria Used by Art Teachers, Art Students, and Artists to Evaluate Works of Art

Previous sections of this chapter discussed sets of criteria art teachers, art students, and artists use to evaluate works of art. These sets may be thought of as banks of criteria from which selections may be made. Selections from the banks may be influenced by the content and aims of the assignment, the reasons the artwork was made, and the purposes for which it is being evaluated. Selections also are subject to change due to increased knowledge or experiences, increased skill development, and the passage of time. Each set of criteria has unique characteristics and qualities. Individuals from within each of these groups—art teachers, art students and artists—ultimately develop their own "personalized" sets of criteria. Criteria in these sets are determined by subjective choice and may or may not require validation from others.

Examination of criteria in sets identified for each of these groups allows for identification of criteria common to all three groups and identification of unique criteria for each of the groups. Such an examination potentially holds meaning for art teachers and preservice preparation of art teachers. Knowledge of similarities and differences in criteria from these sets can influence curriculum, instruction, and, ultimately, the assessment of students' works of art.

Considering the Nature of Evaluation Criteria Identified in Sets

Criteria identified in the sets represent what art teachers, art students, and artists consider valuable in works of art they create and important to their learning about art and development as artists. This is an essential understanding that will shape further discussion of the criteria sets. Portions of criteria from each set can be grouped into art product orientation or artist development orientation clusters. By their nature, the two orientations create a reciprocal relationship. Criteria grouped into the artist development orientation have a direct relationship to works of art; however, that relationship exists in the degree the artworks illustrate the development of the artist. The focus of the criteria is on artistic development. Evidence in works of art acts as a yardstick to measure the artist's development. For example, the criteria "improvement or growth," "personal expression," or "experimentation or risk taking" are more about the artist's development than about the works themselves. Yet, judgments that result from these criteria can only be made through examinations of works of art artists create. Conversely, criteria grouped into the product orientation cluster have a reciprocal relationship with the development of the artist. Criteria in this cluster provide categories—something like a shopping list—from which artists may selectively choose to develop their skill or knowledge. Characteristics found in works of art, as identified by criteria used to evaluate them, are qualitatively judged. The resulting judgments about the quality of the work are based on the quality of the evidence in the work for each criterion as provided by the artist. Hence, improved quality of artwork is the result of development of the artist who created it.

In other words, the types of criteria selected by artists are connected to their concerns about improvement or development as artists, in addition to the physical characteristics of the works they create. To illustrate this point, criteria such as originality, improvement or growth, development of personal style, and development or expansion of previous ideas suggest that artists evaluate works of art in the context of comparing an individual work to others or to the body of work they have created. The traits that exist in individual works of art, such as composition, technical skill with media, effective use of the principles of design, and the elements of art, are important, but the impact these criteria may have in the broader scheme of the artist's development and career appears to be of lesser concern. Artists find themselves in a dilemma when they struggle to find a balance between these two concerns. Certainly, each cluster of criteria is affected by the other, creating a dynamic tension that contributes to the overall development of artists. However, this tension is present to a lesser degree in art classes. For students who want to enter art schools or who wish become artists, the tension may emerge and increase as they come closer to the end of their public schooling. For art teachers, focus on the traits that exist in the work of their students is of more immediate importance for evaluating students' learning, establishing grades, and evaluating curriculum and programs than for tracking of individual or collective growth of students as artists. For many art teachers, keeping the overall development as artists of entire classes of students and the individuals in them at the forefront of evaluation is a challenge. Focusing evaluation of students on their overall development is more challenging for art teachers because of the sheer numbers of classes and students they must teach.

Identifying Similarities and Differences Among Evaluation Criteria Sets

Cross-comparisons of criteria sets used by art teachers, art students, and artists to evaluate artwork reveal a number of similarities and differences among them. Ranked criteria used by art teachers were compared to those used by students at school, students at home, and artists. Criteria related to similar constructs from each of the groups were included in the study (see Table 1.1). Rankings for criteria previously discussed (see Appendixes A, C, D, E) are included for comparison purposes.

The criteria art teachers most frequently reported using to evaluate their students' work were "the elements of art" and "the principles of design." While at school, students also ranked "the elements of art" criterion first; however, when they made artwork at home, this criterion was ranked fourth and artists ranked it ninth. More dramatic differences were found for the criterion "principles of design." Students ranked this criterion 16th while at school and 13th at home; artists ranked it higher, at 10th.

The criterion of "composition or use of space" produced another unique set of rankings. Art teachers ranked it second and artists ranked it third, whereas students ranked it seventh at home and eighth at school.

"Technical skill or craftsmanship" produced relatively high rankings in all groups. Art teachers ranked it fifth, artists ranked it fourth, and students both at home and at school ranked it higher with first and second rankings respectively.

"Personal expression" produced a wide dispersion of rankings. Art teachers ranked it eighth, whereas artists ranked it fourth. Inconsistent rankings resulted for students. At school students ranked personal expression 11th, but ranked it second at home.

"Originality" produced yet another unique distribution of rankings. Whereas artists ranked it first, art teachers and students at school ranked it 10th and students at home ranked it ninth. The criterion "improvement or growth" produced distributions similar to "originality." Artists ranked it second. Students at home ranked it ninth and students at school ranked it 10th. Art teachers ranked it 12th.

Finally, the "experimentation or risk taking" criterion provided wide disagreement among the groups. Artists ranked this criterion fourth, whereas students placed it seventh and eighth at school and at home respectively and art teachers ranked it 16th.

Numerous questions arise about the meaning of these rankings and the distinctive differences of the order of the criteria within the sets. What factors contribute to placements? What rationales support rankings? Do differences in rank orders of criteria have significance for art teachers and art education? In what areas does significance lie? What should art teachers do to account for these differences? Answers to these questions and investigation into issues they raise can affect how art teachers think about assessment and how they conduct assessment of their students' work.

Table 1.1

Comparison of Criteria Most Frequently Used by Art Teachers, Art Students, and Artists to Evaluate Art

Criterion	Art teachers n = 59 % (rank)	Students at school n = 472 % (rank)	Students at home n = 380 % (rank)	Artists n = 50 %(rank)
Elements of art	94.9 (1)	73.9 (1)	60.3 (4)	58.8 (9)
Principles of design	94.9 (1)	42.8 (16)	41.1 (13)	60.0 (10)
Composition or use of space	94.6 (2)	55.8 (8)	50.0 (7)	84.0 (3)
Technical skill or craftsmanship	86.4 (5)	69.7 (2)	64.5 (1)	80.0 (4)
Personal expression ("I did everything the way I wanted it done." "It pleased me.")	83.1 (8)	47.5 (11)	62.1 (2)	80.0 (4)
Originality	79.7 (10)	52.5 (10)	47.1 (9)	90.0 (1)
Attention to details	79.7 (10)	66.1(4)	59.5 (5)	*
Improvement or growth ("I felt I learned something new.")	78.0 (12)	55.3 (9)	44.5 (10)	86.0 (2)
Knowledge of concepts	72.9 (14)	46.8 (13)	43.2 (12)	*
Experimentation or risk taking	67.8 (16)	56.6 (7)	49.5 (8)	80.4 (4)
Safe use of materials and equipment	64.4 (18)	46.0 (15)	34.5 (14)	*
Cognitive processes ("how much this work made me think.")	62.7 (19)	46.2 (14)	43.7 (11)	*

* Criterion not identified by artists.

Relative rankings among criteria suggest different priorities among art teachers, art students, and artists. In general, greater levels of agreement in rankings were found for art teachers and students. To a degree, this may be the result of teacher-imposed criteria for art activities and the resulting artwork. Although directly corresponding rankings were not produced for any criteria across groups, similar relative rankings were produced for a limited group of criteria. For example, "technical skill or craftsmanship" was ranked among the top five criteria in all groups. Knowledge of concepts was ranked between 12th and 14th place among art teachers, students at school, and students at home. Artists did not indicate this criterion in their set. The criterion "safe use of materials and equipment" produced similar rank orders. No other criteria produced similar agreement levels for relative rank ordering of criteria.

Disagreement about relative rank ordering of criteria was common. Examples of this include the relative rankings among groups of the criteria including the elements of art, the principles of design, originality, attention to details, improvement or growth, and experimentation or risk taking. The criterion "elements of art" spanned a range from first for art teachers to ninth for artists. "Principles of art" spanned a range from first for art teachers to 16th for art students. "Originality" spanned a range from first for artists to 10th for art teachers and students at school. "Attention to details" spanned a range from fourth for students to 10th for art teachers. "Improvement or growth" spanned a range from second for artists to 12th for art teachers and "Experimentation or risk taking" ranged from fourth for artists to 16th for art teachers.

Reflections about Assessing Studio Production in Art Education

Disagreement about the rank ordering of criteria sets previously discussed raises a number of issues for art teachers to consider. With increased emphasis on authentic assessment in art education, the question of using assessment criteria similar to those used by professional artists to evaluate their art should not be ignored. Success of authentic assessments depends on assessing authentic products with authentic criteria, that is to say, student artwork should mimic that of professional artists as much as possible, depending on the skill and developmental levels of the students, and it should be assessed with criteria similar to those used by professional artists. This may be valid to a point. Works of art, whether they are made by students of art or by artists, have a number of characteristics in common. They may consist of similar media, subject matter, or themes, stylistic expression, and so on. They also may be made for similar or widely differing purposes. However, assessments must be conducted with specific purposes in mind. If the purposes of assessment and indeed the purposes of art education are at odds with the purposes of assessments of artists, then use of artists' criteria could be invalid. This may sound as if differentiation of artists' criteria and art teachers' criteria is warranted. On the contrary, criteria from both groups may be similar and still serve differing purposes or they may serve the same purposes but include differing criteria. It may be well for art teachers to consider the purposes and criteria artists use to evaluate artwork when selecting criteria to evaluate the work of their students.

Eisner (1998) suggested that schools ought to develop a spectrum of literacies that enable students to participate in and find meaning through the major forms from which meaning has been constituted. He contended that programs schools provide, what is emphasized or minimized, and what is assigned prime time and what is excluded reflect the directions in which we believe children should grow. If we do not emphasize the things artists consider important, such as the purposes of their evaluations and their evaluation criteria, and if we do not consider them important to similar degrees as artists do, then we are not providing the guidance and knowledge to help children grow in the direction we believe they should grow. Through increased emphasis on criteria used by artists to evaluate their work, art teachers contribute to expanding the artistic literacy of their students.

Eisner (1998) further contended that each child should be given programs and opportunities to play to their strengths and to pursue and exploit meaning systems for which they have special aptitudes or interests. Children who make art at home are expressing their unique interests or aptitudes for making art. Because evaluation criteria sets used at home by students differ from those used in school and from those used by the art teacher, art teachers may be preventing students from playing to their strengths and developing their special aptitudes and interests. Art teachers are confronted with the dilemma of educating students about the essential content of art education and developing their skills while keeping the special aptitudes and interests of the students in mind. Art teachers should examine differences in criteria priorities suggested by students both in school and at home and consider the reasons for these differences and their relationship to the differing purposes for which art teachers teach art and for which students make art. Amending and reprioritizing the criteria set used to evaluate studio products made in school may lead to more student engagement and increased achievement in art education programs.

Feldman (1980) contended that the student should be given greater control over what will be learned and how it will be learned. He recommended that, if education is to better fulfill its mission, the relationship to knowledge must be reconceptualized in a model he called "the child as craftsman." Feldman suggested that the child-as-craftsman model requires educators to view children as people who want to be good at something. The child craftsman continually wants to take pride in accomplishments and build a sense of integrity about his or her own work. The aim of the child-as-craftsman model is not to suggest that young children are predestined to find satisfaction with a particular field or discipline, but rather that the function of education should be to engage the child in pursuit of mastery of a satisfying craft or crafts and to find work to do that is likely to bring adult satisfaction, fulfillment, and expression.   To accomplish these results, art teachers should consider how assessments include evaluation of the overall development of their students as artists and increase emphasis on developing the child as craftsman.   This notion represents a shift from emphasis on the work of art as evidence of development to a broader examination of factors that contribute to the overall development of the student as an artist or consumer of art.   Designing activities and selecting assessment criteria compatible with such activities will lead art teachers to reexamine the goals of their programs and the indicators or criteria that will provide evidence that students have raised their level of achievement and increased their development as artists.

Engaging students in learning that can increase the emphasis on development of the child as artist and that can foster their development as artists provides unique challenges to art teachers. Csikszentmihalyi and Schneider (2000) studied teenagers and their preparation for entering the world of work. They reported that students spent only 54% of their school day in optimal learning experiences that were interactive and engaging.   The remainder of students' time was spent in passive attending to information transmitted to the entire class.   Students found school activities either challenging or enjoyable, but not both. Students rarely felt that activities emphasizing enjoyment were viewed as essential in achieving future goals. They revealed that activities that were challenging and required more concentration were more important in formulating future goals.   Students reported that activities in which they were actively engaged in learning were more important to achieving their future goals. Csikszentmihalyi and Schneider contended that "all such activities require students to engage in problem solving tasks with clear objectives and challenge them to use their abilities to demonstrate their understanding of the subject matter" (p. 149). Furthermore they suggested that the best activities were those that balance challenge with high levels of skill and concentration. Such activities must have clearly identified purposes that lead to higher engagement. For art teachers, this means that students must be given rigorous tasks that require problem-solving skills and concentration. Such activities must be supported with clear purposes and evaluated with an array of criteria that match the stated purposes.

In order to successfully achieve these ends, art teachers must seek a new conceptualization of curriculum and assessment that provides a better balance among knowledge of discipline content and skills, student interests, and needs of the field. In designing such an art education program, teachers need to focus on assessment criteria, being careful to reorder and align them with the purposes and objectives of their programs and those of students and artists. Such restructuring will lead art teachers to a more comprehensive assessment of learning and of the artistic development of students.

Study Questions

1. Describe three major developments from the history of assessment in the arts. How have these events affected the nature of art education? What positive influences have they had? What negative influences have they had?
2. Review the drawbacks and positive effects assessment has had on art education. Discuss the effects. How can the drawbacks be addressed to improve learning and assessments? How can the positive effects be expanded and their positive impact magnified?
3. Examine criteria art teachers use to evaluate students' studio production. What criteria do you use to evaluate students' studio work? What similarities and differences among criteria can you identify?
4. Compare criteria art teachers and artists use to evaluate studio work. What differences and similarities can you identify? What possible reasons can you provide to explain the similarities and differences you identify?
5. Examine differences between criteria students use to evaluate artwork they make in school and artwork they make at home. What reasons can you provide to explain the similarities and differences you identify?

References

Armsrong, C. L. (1994). *Designing assessment in art.* Reston, VA: National Art Education Association.

Beattie, D. K. (1997). *Assessment in art education.* Worchester, MA: Davis Publications.

Calderone, J., King, L. M., & Horkay, N. (Eds.). (1997). The NAEP guide (NCES Publication No. 97-990). Washington, DC: U.S. Department of Education, National Center for Educational Statistics.

Chittendon, E. (1991). Authentic assessment, evaluation, and documentation of student performance. In V. Perrone (Ed.), *Expanding student assessment* (pp. 22–31). Alexandria, VA: Association for Supervision and Curriculum Development.

Cronbach, L. J. (1960). *Essentials of psychological testing* (3rd ed.). New York: Harper & Row.

Csikszentmihalyi, M., & Schneider, B. (2000). *Becoming adult: How teenagers prepare for the world of work.* New York: Basic Books.

Diket, R. M., Burton, D., & Sabol, F. R. (2000). Taking another look: Secondary analysis of the NAEP report card in visual arts. *Studies in Art Education, 41*(3), 202–207.

Eisner, E. W. (1998). *The kind of schools we need: Personal essays.* Portsmouth, NH: Heinemann.

Feldman, D. H. (1980). *Beyond universals in cognitive development.* Norwood, NJ: Ablex.

Improving America's Schools Act of 1994, H.R. 6, 103d Cong. 2nd Sess.

Mueller, D. J. (1986). *Measuring social attitudes.* New York: Teachers College Press.

Music Educators National Conference. (1994). *National standards for arts education: What every young American should know and be able to do in the arts.* Reston, VA: Author.

National Commission on Excellence in Education. (1983). *A nation at risk.* Washington, DC: U.S. Government Printing Office.

National Endowment for the Arts. (1988). *Toward civilization: Overview from the report on arts education.* Washington, DC: Author.

Persky, H. R., Sandene, B. A., & Askew, J. M. (1999). *The NAEP 1997 arts report card: Eighth grade findings from the national assessment of educational progress.* Washington, DC: U.S. Department of Education, Office of Educational Research and Improvement.

Sabol, F. R. (1990). Toward development of a visual arts diagnostic achievement test: Issues and concerns. In M. Zurmuehlen (Ed.), *Working papers in art education, 1989–1990* (pp. 78-85). Iowa City, IA: The School of Art and Art History of the University of Iowa.

Sabol, F. R. (1994). A critical examination of visual arts achievement tests from state departments of education in the United States. *Dissertation Abstracts International, 56,* (2A), 9518525. (University Microfilms No. 5602A).

Sabol, F. R. (1998a). *Needs assessment and identification of urban art teachers in the western region of the national art education association.* Reston, VA: The National Art Education Foundation.

Sabol, F. R. (1998b). What are we testing?: Content analysis of state visual arts achievement tests. *Visual Arts Research,* 24 (1), 1–12.

Sabol, F. R. (1999a). *Needs assessment and identification of rural art teachers in the western region of the national art education association.* Reston, VA: The National Art Education Foundation.

Sabol, F. R. (1999b, March). *What do art teachers think about assessment in art education?* Paper presented at the national convention of the National Art Education Association, Washington, DC.

Sabol, F. R. (2001a). *Reaching out to rural and urban art teachers in the western region of the national art education association: Needs assessment and identification of new members.* Reston, VA: National Art Education Foundation.

Sabol, F. R. (2001b). *Regional findings from a secondary analysis of the 1997 NAEP art assessment based on responses to creating and responding exercises.* Studies in Art Education, 43(1), 18–34.

Sabol, F. R., & Bensur, B. (2000, March). *What attitudes do art teachers hold about assessment in art education?* Paper presented at the national convention of the National Art Education Association, Los Angeles, CA.

Sabol, F. R., & Zimmerman, E. (1997). *An introduction: Standardized testing and authentic assessment research in art education.* In S. D. La Pierre & E. Zimmerman (Eds.), Research methods and methodologies for art education (pp. 137–169). Reston, VA: National Art Education Association.

Shuler, S. C., & Connealy, S. (1998). *The evolution of state arts assessment: From Sisyphus to stone soup.* Arts Education Policy Review, 100 (issue 1), 12–19.

Thurstone, L. L. (1928). Attitudes can be measured. *American Journal of Sociology*, 33, 529–554.

Thurstone, L. L. (1931). The measurement of social attitudes. *Journal of Abnormal and Social Psychology*, 26, 249–269.

U.S. Department of Education (1991). *America 2000: An education strategy.* Washington, DC: U.S. Government Printing Office.

U.S. Department of Education (1994). *Goals 2000: Educate America Act.* Washington, DC: U.S. Government Printing Office.

ALTERNATIVE ASSESSMENT STRATEGIES FOR SCHOOLS

In chapter 1, the results of the project survey of artists, art teachers, and students suggest that the teacher's perception of K–12 learning outcomes differs significantly from what artists and K–12 students seek to achieve. Although 90% of the teachers surveyed considered the elements and principles of design to be essential in learning art, both artists and students thought that "getting better at making art" should be the most important goal in art learning. Standardized tests also encourage the development of tests that are empirically based, including knowledge of elements and principles rather than strategies that measure expressive outcomes, such as the aesthetic quality of the art products and visual problem-solving abilities. Consequently, standardized assessment models may not be the best answers or "quick fixes" for improving instruction and raising student achievement. The variance between the goals set by art teachers and by artists and students, as well as other concerns, make a strong case for designing alternative art evaluation instruments and techniques for assessing expressive content more closely related to the nature of the artistic process.

The need, as we view it, is to develop a number of different alternative evaluation instruments and strategies that provide hard data but are not in the form of the standard paper-and-pencil multiple-choice tests now being used in most testing programs. What we advocate are assessment instruments that support proven methods in the visual arts and also take advantage of all the newer imaging technology. What we have attempted to do in this project is to utilize the technology and imaging programs that were not available a decade ago, such as digital cameras and multimedia computer programs. The rationale for using the electronic portfolio as an assessment device came from the recognition that we now have the capabilities to apply these tools in the evaluation of large groups of students. Furthermore, the costs of implementing programs of this type are now within the reach of school budgets and these programs are also simple enough that teachers and students may use them without facing a steep learning curve. In the project, we combined tested, validated portfolio assessment techniques in the visual arts and incorporated them into electronic formats so that they might have applicability to assessing larger numbers of students. The project also addressed the need to conduct further research studies on the assessment of expressive learning using formative or authentic evaluation techniques that can apply to K–12 learning.

The Politics of the Assessment Process

"Testing mania" may be an appropriate phrase for describing the current climate and context for assessment in our schools. State assessment programs are the devices that legislatures, school administrators, and the general public use to gauge school performance and success. Consequently, test scores have become front-page news and schools' quality and worth are being judged by test scores, which are reported to various populations on a regular basis. School superintendents have taken to the idea of "report cards" to the public on the performance of their school systems. Such reports give data to the general public based on student performance in the areas of reading, mathematics, and science as indicators of the quality of education. School boards have entered into contracts with administrators and teachers that provide incentives, such as bonuses for improvement in critical reading and math test scores. Wage increases for teachers may become dependent on test scores. Even with this accelerated pace of mass testing, the questions that still remain unanswered are whether learning within schools has increased and whether the students have acquired the skills or competencies necessary to be considered literate. The arts have not been left out of the assessment movement and, in many states, art testing programs are being designed or implemented. However, at last count, fewer than 25% of states are developing arts assessment components for their testing programs.

Most educators would agree that evaluation is an important part of the educational process, but it is too important to restrict the process to standardized tests as the only indicator of student learning or success in an academic program. Further assessment programs, when generated from the top down, have a significant effect on the content of curriculum and instructional time in the school day that is directed toward reading and mathematical skills, especially in the primary grades. Consequently, because of the testing mania, more school systems want to perform well on the tests to ease the pedagogical or political pressures that they face in today's educational environment. The rational voice in education would agree that mass testing is not a positive development in public education, but it now exists and each discipline, including art, must address the consequences, especially in the area of curriculum content and design.

The Competition to Perform

The term performance, related to school programs, is usually associated with athletics and arts programs. However, today, with the emphasis on academic performance in such core subjects as math and reading, the competition has shifted from the gridiron and the stage to the classroom. Schools are being held responsible for student performance as measured by test scores in all academic areas. In larger urban areas that contain many school districts of varying quality and financial support, the competition between the schools is growing each year and causing a variety of problems. For example, it is well known that in the Chicago area families with children who are buying homes rate good schools as a dominant criterion when choosing a neighborhood. Real estate agents are very cognizant of their priority. They use high test scores as a measure of school success and as a marketing ploy to attract people to their home listings in quality school districts. Furthermore, in the school districts that have low test scores, not only is the real estate market affected, but the reward system for personnel in the schools is also being affected. Teachers are being told that they must perform well on tests especially in the core subjects of reading and mathematics. The scores are published as front-page news in most states. Television regularly reports the test scores as it would box scores for sports events. Raises are being tied to test scores for administrators and teachers within districts. The new federal legislation may connect student test scores over time to continuations of federal funding. The competitive climate has changed how teachers, students, and administrations interact among themselves, with their school boards, and with the general public. Teachers are put under enormous stress in today's classrooms, especially in those grade levels that are used for testing purposes such as the third or fourth grade in elementary testing. Teachers openly complain about the amount of class time that they must take in preparing their students for tests and also about the fears and anxieties created by not having their students perform at an acceptable level. It is not enough to equal the test scores of previous years: What is being called for in most cases is a significant increase each year in the performance of students in the core subjects.

Of even more concern is the fact that schools are becoming desperate and their personnel are using a variety of ways to improve student performance on the tests, some of which are unethical and dishonest. School systems and individual teachers and administrators have been caught cheating by supplying information about the tests to students. Schools are controlling attendance on days that the test is administered: students who will not perform well are discouraged from attending or diverted to other activities in the school, rather than taking the test and performing poorly. Eliminating students who have performed poorly from the tests should send a message to the administration, and to legislators, that they have gone too far in using test scores to assess student performance. We can go on with this litany of sins of assessment, but to what end? Mandated testing programs are dramatically changing the climate of schools and these changes are not for the better. It is time to consider alternatives to the mass testing of students.

Relationship Between Evaluation and Assessment and the Curriculum

The purpose of this chapter is to discuss the relationship between mass testing as a means of evaluation of school and student performance and how this process may affect or drive the curriculum. The dilemma is whether to design curriculum and then evaluate it based on criteria and techniques applicable to its content or based on its design evaluation devices, which dictate the content.

As far as firsthand experience in evaluation processes and techniques of programs and curriculum goes, the authors collectively have had more direct experience in school assessment programs than most in art education. Stanley Madeja working with the JDR 3rd Fund and the Aesthetic Education Program in the 1970s, provides one example of school-based evaluation models that build assessment as an integral part of the curriculum development process. In 1968, a program was started in the University City Public Schools in Missouri that initiated what is now called the Arts in Education Movement in this country. The project had two major components: curriculum development in the arts and teacher training for the purpose of designing and implementing a general education program for all the arts.

In the early stages of the project, it became evident in the designing of a basal arts curriculum for all students that traditional quantitative techniques for curriculum evaluation were not at all appropriate for assessing art activities in the classroom. This led to the necessity for developing new methods by which a record could be created of what happens in the classroom when arts activities are being taught. The evaluation of the Arts in General Education Project was conducted by a team headed by Jack Davis (Davis, Thuernau, Hudgens, & Hall, 1971–1973), whose purpose was to observe and document the development of a new arts curriculum and arts program throughout an entire school system. The evaluation team was concerned with four areas: a detailed description of the progress of the curriculum project, identification and isolation of factors contributing to success or failure of the project, development of methods and instruments for evaluating the arts instructional units and curriculum, and small experimental and descriptive studies. It should be noted that the evaluation of the Arts in General Education Project developed methods and techniques for assessing student activities and curriculum and for monitoring the overall progress of the project. The techniques originally designed and tested in actual class-rooms in the Arts in General Education evaluation later were used in the Aesthetic Education Program (Madeja & Onuska, 1977) evaluation. These projects plowed new ground in evaluation. The basic premise was simple. Curriculum development was an interactive, step-by-step process that comprised defining the content and activities for teaching that content, observing and making judgments about the success of the classroom activity, and then revising or even redefining the content or activities based on the classroom experience. The principle was that the evaluation was not separate from the curriculum development, but rather an integral part of the total developmental cycle. The person conducting the evaluation was just as much a part of the curriculum development team as the person writing the curriculum. The information that was gathered was for the purpose of improving the curriculum content, developing assessment techniques, and improving classroom activities. It was no accident that over time the evaluator and the teacher curriculum writer became closely connected.

The Aesthetic Education Program evaluation process was based on the use of trained observers who carried out an exhaustive observational monitoring of an entire unit of instructional materials from beginning to end. This information, fed back to the development staff, served as a basis for revision and further trials of the curriculum materials. Hall and Thuernau (1975) documented the methods in their summary of the formative evaluation procedures of the Aesthetic Education Program. They described the relationship between evaluation techniques and the development of curriculum in a classroom setting. At the end of this stage, the curriculum materials met three major review criteria in order to be considered evaluated: First, they must have been in keeping with the overall goal of the curriculum; second, there must be evidence that the curriculum unit could stand alone in the hands of a competent teacher and be successfully implemented without additional aid, beyond that given in the Teachers' Guide; and third, the curriculum unit must have met certain short-term objectives, demonstrated by verification of measurable differences between students who had studied the units and those who had not.

Does Assessment Drive the Curriculum?

A number of related studies conducted at that time contributed to clarifying this methodology. Smith and Geoffrey (1968) investigated the classroom form and its social structure and developed a methodology termed "classroom ethnography" to accomplish this. It called for direct observation of classroom instruction, on a preselected topic, by a trained observer who did not become a participant in the instructional process. Later, Robert Stake (1976) approached this problem by developing a methodology he called "response evaluation," which encompassed some of the same characteristics. Response evaluation in Stake's definition was "an alternative, an old alternative, based on what people do naturally to evaluate things they observe and react to" (p.14). He said that this kind of evaluation had been avoided in district, state, and federal planning documents and regulations because it is subjective and poorly suited to formal contracts. He defined an educational evaluation as a "responsive" evaluation if it was oriented more directly to program activities than to program intents, if it responded to audience requirements for information, and if the different value perspectives present were referred to in reporting the success or failure of the program. The evaluation models that were developed in the University City Arts Project and then later in the Aesthetic Education Program inserted (or introduced) evaluation into the curriculum design process. The methodologies for evaluation varied, but the basic premise was that the two entities, curriculum design or development and evaluation, had to be related and the relationship should be determined by the content of the curriculum being assessed.

State-Wide Testing Programs and Their Effects on the Curriculum

Now let us contrast the interactive curriculum development approach with state art assessment programs. The testing program at state or school district levels has traditionally been more diagnostic than summative. By diagnostic, we mean schools would administer standardized tests at different grade levels to determine whether students compared favorably with another grade level group, based on national or regional norms. Reading and mathematics have been the most prominent areas for in-school testing programs with standardized achievement tests such as the Iowa Test of Basic Skills. However, a significant switch of philosophy and design took place when state-wide testing programs were initiated that, in most venues, have no relationship to the school-based diagnostic testing. Performance-based assessment of basic reading and mathematics skills has become the main direction of state-wide testing. As discussed in the introduction, the rationale for the state assessment programs is politically rather than pedagogically based. Assessment has become fashionable, but not because of a school's need to assess the effectiveness of teaching or to improve learning. Quite to the contrary, what schools are confronting is a political crisis in education. Schools are being condemned as ineffective. American education, in terms of its overall design and framework, was and is being challenged in a way it has never been challenged before, with the charge that it is not delivering an acceptable product. Consequently, the "quick fix" for states and local districts is to instigate a comprehensive incremental assessment program that would assess performance in basic skills at specific grade levels, usually at three-year intervals such as the third, sixth, ninth, and eleventh grade levels.

Madeja (2002, p1) described a personal experience in Missouri when the state-wide BEST TEST, an acronym for Basic Educational Skills Test, was introduced in the 1970s:

> I will never forget the first year the test was administered. I opened the St. Louis Dispatch news-paper and on the front page, in one inch high headlines,the paper noted that students statewide had failed the BEST Test, with many of the better schools scoring below the 50th percentile. This was not the predicted result by most educators as they anticipated that the test scores would be high and consequently, they could justify their school excellence based on the scores. (To make matters worse, the test was not very difficult.) The low scores created an embarrassing situation for the schools; however, a miracle happened. The test was given the following spring, one year later, and miraculously all the students in Missouri improved dramatically in that one year. In some school systems, the gains were thirty to forty percent. Now these not only were significant gains, but unbelievable gains and anyone who has been educated in either the right or left brain could easily figure out what happened. The teachers and the school system were not going to get blind-sided again by a statewide testing program. They started to coach the students early in the year as to the content of tests and as a result the curriculum of most schools [was] altered dramatically in order for the schools to "teach for the test." (p. 1)

The scenario in Missouri continues to happen more subtly in schools and states that now have assessment programs at the state or school district level. The reading scores in some schools are improving. Whether Johnny and Sally are reading any better today than they did 15 years ago is hard to determine, but we feel very comfortable in saying that the assessment program at the state and local level is having a significant effect on curriculum development. Moreover, it is having a significant effect on what content is presented and which disciplines are taught within the schools. More and more of the school day, especially in school systems that deal with at-risk students or students who need remedial work, is spent trying to teach students to read. However, the literacy rate in schools even with intensive reading and writing programs is not dramatically increasing.

The Negative and Positive Effects of the Top-Down Evaluation Model

Based on the results so far, should we abandon state-wide testing? Not at all. The state-wide programs do offer an opportunity to provide baseline data in critical subjects on student performance. Madeja (1978) argued in the late 1970s that there was a need for standardized instruments for assessing the arts, applicable to different age levels in schools. The author's position is that any kind of standardized test should be developed with diagnostic instruments that are designed to mesh with the existing school-based testing program and the curriculum. Unlike European countries such as Germany, France, and the Netherlands, which have centralized national educational systems, each state has hundreds of school districts that act as small city-states and have control of the design and content of their own curriculum. Thus, great variances exist between school districts, as there is no standardization of the curriculum or instructional strategies in art or other subjects by state agencies. Consequently, it is difficult to use standardized measures as the only assessment of student performance and progress in a given subject area. Technologies are now available that could be used as the basis for sophisticated and relatively economical instrumentation for assessing knowledge in all subject areas, including the arts. If resources and talent were allocated to the task, diagnostic instruments or tests to determine individual student strengths and weaknesses in the visual arts domain could be designed to become one part of the in-school grade-level testing programs. Such instruments in the visual arts would assess student abilities and knowledge in such categories as art appreciation, sensory organization and planning, sensory recall and reproduction, art vocabulary and art techniques, art skills, art history; conscious and unconscious preferences and interests in aesthetic phenomena, and attitudes toward art and aesthetics. These instruments would provide a longitudinal record of student performance and skills in art, additional information beyond test scores, regional and national norms at the different grade levels based on what is being taught, and an alternative model or plan for student progress.

The Need for Alternate Models for School-Based Assessment

Standardized instruments need to be developed for grade-level testing to be used at the state and local levels. Akin to what is now happening in many states, art has not had an accepted national or regional standardized test that is used to develop any kind of normative data for the visual arts in studio competencies, critical analysis, or knowledge of art history. One of the key reasons why the visual arts have lagged in test development is that there are very few standardized curricula in the visual arts and no general consensus about the content of the K–12 visual arts program. Nonetheless, states are now implementing state-wide assessment programs in art. They are addressing the problem of standardized testing in art, but still are handicapped by the lack of standardized art content or curriculum in art.

Therefore, curriculum development in art and state-wide testing in art must be connected in order to make the assessment programs successful. More use of the formative evaluation techniques described in this text should be incorporated into state-wide assessment programs. Curricula and student learning in the visual arts need to be assessed. State-wide curriculum development efforts that include formative evaluation techniques should precede state-wide test development. This would be the ideal model for evaluation, that is, to have a defined, tested art curriculum in place before we develop state-wide tests. If this were accomplished, art tests as part of state programs would make more sense. So, it is necessary to put the horse before the cart and integrate evaluation into the curriculum development process in art and, when the "tested curriculum" is in place, then let us develop the summative measures, or state-wide art testing, that assess the content. If this process took place, the proper tail would be wagging the proper dog or, more appropriately, the dog would be wagging his or her own tail.

Alternative Models for Assessment of Expressive Learning in the Visual Arts

Art teachers have been hesitant to use assessment devices such as art tasks for evaluating student performance and for program evaluation. However, there is a consensus among art teachers that the art product, such as a painting or sculpture, that a student actually creates in a classroom setting can be used as the basis for grading and assessing student performance in studio-oriented art programs. The idea that frightens or threatens the art teacher is the suggestion that these products the students produce can be quantified. Why this negative reaction to quantification? One reason many teachers are concerned that creative or expressive work cannot be quantified in any meaningful way is that an interpretation or judgment would be too subjective. Another is that creative, boundary-breaking initiatives could be stifled or negated because of students' desire to receive a high grade. Students might also choose more conventional routes in their production of art, instead of taking risks. Another is the student-oriented concern that many students enroll in art classes because they are not finding success or satisfaction in other classes. Thus, there is concern that quantification,which implies some more academic rigor, may discourage students from taking elective art courses, especially in high school. So, quantification of art products in the art program, especially at the senior high level where most of the sophisticated studio programs reside, is suspect and is not well accepted by art teachers.

Quantifying Art Products in the Art Classroom

All art programs produce visual products and art teachers can and do judge the quality and the technical attributes of these works regularly in giving the student a grade. Teachers will admit that they use the art product as a criterion for determining a grade, but they also integrate such things as level of effort, the uniqueness of the concept of the visual product, and the deportment or classroom behavior of the student to determine student progress and success in art. However, the assessment question is not whether these products can be used in evaluating student performance or learning in the art program. Rather, the questions are how can they be used as evidence of student performance and how can they be used as indicators of student progress over time in such areas as visual perception, aesthetic decision-making, critical analysis, visual problem solving, and studio competencies? Can a data collection system be developed using art products generated from the classroom activities that trace students' development over time through the products they develop? In art education, there has been a century of development and use of student products as assessment data. In the early part of the century, drawing scales were used for evaluating students' drawing. The Goodenough Harris Draw, a Man-Women-Self-Portrait test battery, uses preschool childrens' drawings to assess general intelligence and has developed visual rubrics and scales that the teacher can use for scoring student performance. This test has 75 years of cross-cultural data and protocols for scoring that transcend cultural groups. In a period from 1913 to 1946, 28 other art tests were developed and 15 of the tests were published for use in school (Kintner, 1933) (Madeja, 1959).

The Portfolio as an Alternative Assessment Instrument

By definition, a portfolio is "a portable case for carrying newspapers, prints, or art works." The term has also been related to accounting practices and organization of information as being an itemized account of an investment organization, bank, or individual investor. The term folio, a subset of portfolio, is usually associated with a grouping of papers in some orderly fashion, such as a folio of photographs, a folio of prints, or a drawing folio. All of these definitions and the use of the terms folio and portfolio suggest a functional and metaphorical organization of information. Organizing visual information into folio formats is not a new enterprise. Historically, there have been countless examples. The most familiar are the notebooks and folios of Leonardo DaVinci and the extended and detailed notebooks and drawings of Charles Darwin (1979). Both of these intellectual giants of the last millennium used observation techniques to explain the phenomena that they were studying. Darwin was never considered an artist and yet many of his notebooks have detailed drawings of the natural phenomena he studied. The flora and fauna of various environs in the world were recorded in this fashion. Later, these portfolios were used as the basis for his definitive work, Origin of Species published in 1859 (Darwin 1979). DaVinci was an artist, scientist, engineer, and physiologist. He used artistic skills to visually record his ideas and theories about anatomy, bronze casting, works of art, machines, described in the Codex Madrid I and II Reti, 1965.   Art teachers have been using portfolio techniques at every level. Elementary art teachers create a portfolio for the work of every student, sometimes numbering in the hundreds of works, which they review at the end of each grading period. High school teachers have students save their work for at least the semester as a portfolio. At the college level, portfolios are used today as an entry-and-exit requirement for many of the art programs at colleges, universities, and independent art schools. The Advanced Placement Program in studio art uses an art portfolio as a part of the data the student is required to present for entry into the program. The International Baccalaureate Program and the Advanced Placement Program use the portfolio as evidence of the student's accomplishments and success in a high-school-level art program. It is well known in the design field that a student who is graduating from a school of art must have a portfolio that he or she can show to prospective employers. In art education, studio and professional portfolios now are part of the graduation requirement for many programs that educate art teachers. Thus, the portfolio has had a long tradition in the visual arts as an evaluation instrument to record student accomplishments.

Most of the portfolios that students create are reviewed and graded by an art teacher. Quantification and grading of these portfolios has never been an exacting science. They are usually reviewed by a group of faculty who attempt to reach a consensus on the quality of the products contained in the portfolio. To the authors' knowledge, there have been few attempts to use a formalized grading system in judging portfolios. Portfolios are usually judged on a pass-fail basis and are accompanied by a narrative by the reviewing group as to the student's success. So, we might argue that quantification of artworks is already going on, but that the methodology and techniques used might be too subjective. Should this, however, prevent us from attempting to quantify art products from the portfolio as a body of work? The authors suggest that this should not be an issue and that art teachers with appropriate training at all levels are capable of judging the artistic aesthetic merits of artworks using well-established techniques in the field. This was demonstrated in the studies described in this text where the art teacher judgments of student artworks were reliable at the .01 level, which indicates 99% or better agreement as to the quality of the artworks. The case studies described in Chapter 5 demonstrate that art teachers need not fear stifling the creative and artistic thinking in their classrooms by introducing quantification methodology in the assessment process. The elementary school case studies integrated the adjudication techniques of the students' work into the portfolios and into the grading system. The portfolio can take many forms. What follows is a brief description of different portfolio formats.

Journal portfolio. The written journal is probably the oldest form of what we are now calling a portfolio. Journaling, which is now the popular term, implies an active state by the writer. These techniques have been used successfully in writing, literature, and criticism classes in colleges and high school English programs. The dominant characteristic of the journals is their emphasis on the linguistic base for describing and providing evidence that students are learning the content. It also implies that some analysis and interpretation of the content of a course of study is taking place and suggests that students should be introspective and react through language about their attitudes and conceptualization of the course content. Journals can be very structured and teacher-directed, or they can be open-ended. The recent anthology of writings edited by Bonnie Sunstein and Jonathan Lovell (2000) is an excellent overview of the status of using language-based portfolios as an evaluation tool.

A teacher's portfolio or log. The simplest method of teacher self-evaluation is to keep a log that systematically records happenings in the classroom. This is a record of the teacher's impression or assessments of student art performance and how well the objectives of the instructional programs are being met. A log is a time-consuming portfolio technique because only the teacher collects the data. An alternative is to involve the student as part of the data collecting system. Some portfolio designs that include student data collection are described at the end of this chapter.

Items for the student portfolio/or log would include:

1. Student work, such as writings, artwork, audio or video recordings, and photographs of their classroom accomplishments,
2. Teacher assessments of the student's performance on various classroom art tasks based on rubrics developed in the project,
3. Records of the student's performance on controlled and noncontrolled art tasks, such as drawings, paintings, and designs.

Controlled Task Portfolio. This portfolio format has the student organize the visual information in a logical sequence with the design of the visual information being part of the problem. The difference between this format and the traditional portfolio is that portfolios used in the controlled task approach are used to assess student accomplishments over time. These tasks can be given to the whole class in advance. The tasks measure progress over time on specific studio skills or techniques the teacher feels are important in appreciating the artwork or understanding the artist. For example, if the portfolio is used as a record of student accomplishments in a figure drawing class, there could be a pre-and post-controlled task of a drawing problem using the human figure. The students would be asked to draw the model using the same pose with the same media two times, once at the beginning of the course and once at the end. This would be a limited use of a controlled task. A variation would be to have a number of different controlled tasks that the student would do of the figure over the time frame of the course. Thus, the teacher could look at the students' progress using the same assignments over time.

International Baccalaureate Schools portfolio. The International Baccalaureate Program has adopted the use of the portfolio as an assessment device in many areas of study, including art (see web site ibo.org). The format applicable to the visual arts is a relatively open-ended portfolio requirement that the student is asked to prepare in his or her final year. The program has published a set of images that act as end states for studio artwork at the senior-high level. The program defines these exemplars of student artwork not as rubrics, but rather as achievement levels that high-school-age students can attain in the studio arts.

The Advanced Placement portfolio in the visual arts. The Advanced Placement Program is designed to achieve the advanced placement of high school students at the college level and has been in existence for about 30 years. In the studio areas, high school students are required to prepare a portfolio of slides and original work reflecting their accomplishments in art in both two- and three-dimensional work. They are also required to write an artist statement about the intent and direction of their work and about their philosophy of art. The portfolio should represent a body of work that students have created, usually in their junior and senior years of high school. Walter Askin (Askin, 1985), the Chief and Reader for the Advanced Placement Studio Component, describes the process as follows:

> The requirements for the advanced placement portfolios are determined by the Development Committee in Studio Art and are judged by a nationwide group of artists and visual arts teachers from colleges and secondary schools. Portfolio requirements have changed in focus and emphasis over the years. The Development Committee in Studio Art meets periodically to make revisions so that the portfolio requirements are current. This is done with the advice and assistance of test specialists from Educational Testing Service and the Chief Reader in Studio Art; comments and suggestions from current advanced placement teachers are also carefully considered. (p.7)

Similar formats to those described previously are being used in a variety of ways by teachers at all levels in K–12 schools. They speak to the utility of the portfolio as an alternative or as an addition to the standardized testing programs used in most of our states. It is really necessary, however, to reaffirm that testing is not a dirty word and the authors agree that standards and testing should be used in assessing K–12 schools. However, standardized tests cannot and should not be the only measure used, especially in arts assessment (See Fig. 5.3 in Chapter 5, which is a sample Advanced Placement portfolio).

Electronic Portfolio Assessment Design

The Madeja Visual Modeling of Information System (MVMIS) was the format used to develop the design of multimedia portfolios in the project's research at Northern Illinois Univerisity on the feasibility of the electronic portfolio as an alternative assessment device for visual learning. Paolo Soleri, architect, stated that "time is a symbolic means of measuring" (1999). Reflecting Soleri, the MVMIS is designed to assist in the development of an evaluation instrument for collecting information that includes a defined time frame over the duration of a learning experience. The electronic portfolios using this data collection system provide an assessment system that:
- Is a data-collecting activity in an electronic portfolio format, where the evaluation and interpretation of the data are based on the user design and where the user is responsible for the documenting of information.
- Requires the user to arrange a knowledge base that emphasizes and encourages connecting concepts and ideas to the knowledge streams of the data collected.

- Has the potential of creating a multimedia database incorporating the content choices that the user designs.
- Is an independent assessment instrument based on the mapping, tracking, analyzing, interpreting, and evaluating the information collected by the user.
- Is a data collection system and assessment process formed through the collaborative activity of the user, the teacher, and the institution.

Assumptions About the Process of Visual Modeling

There is a natural need for humans to record events, ideas, concepts, data, and, in more than one sense modality, and it can be assumed that there is a positive interface between data generated in each of the sense modalities: verbal, visual, auditory, kinetic, and olfactory. Furthermore, the translation, synthesis, juxtaposition, and combining of sense modalities such as language and image contribute to the comprehension of knowledge. The acquiring, organizing, and collecting of knowledge can be a linear process, but the path also may be nonlinear, spiral, serpentine, or circular. Whatever visual configuration is used in the tracking and documenting process may include more than one information stream and has no commitment to one set of organizing principles.

The modeling experience organizes data in one or more sense modalities into a coherent "whole," where a portfolio becomes the documentation of what has been learned over a defined time frame. Within that time frame, the user or the teacher determines the points of interaction in the information streams where the user can interpret or analyze the data or information collected. These are called "modes of analysis and interpretation." As such, they are synthesizing experiences or products that can be accessed by the user and a teacher, parent, or educational institution. They are also the keystones to evaluating the user's progress over a defined time frame, such as a degree program, project, or course of study. The interaction modes are building blocks to creating the portfolio as a culminating experience. In summary, the process by which the user organizes and explains the knowledge streams base is a documentation of what has been learned. The portfolio becomes the record of that process, the user's reflection, analysis, interpretation, and judgment of the process, and the record for determining what has been learned.

The Process of Visual Modeling of Information

The parts of the model that make up the process of information modeling include: the Acquisition of Knowledge stream; a multisensory database; the Reaction stream, and the Interaction Zone with Modes of Analysis and Interpretation; and the culminating experience in the portfolio itself. The modeling activity in this system includes the development of visual formats or multimedia formats by which users can document the content and knowledge they are acquiring over a given time frame. Visual

Madeja's Knowledge System Fig. 2.1

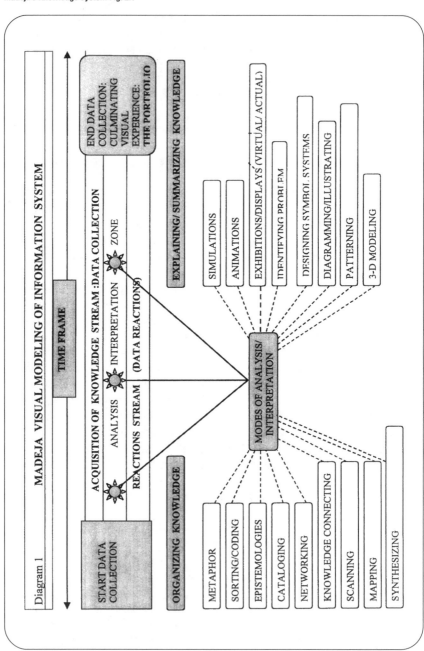

Diagram 1 — MADEJA VISUAL MODELING OF INFORMATION SYSTEM

modeling should take place in the acquisition stream, analysis interpetation zone, and reaction stream where the user is attempting to bring together knowledge streams and show the connections and relationships that exist between them. Modeling also implies that there is a software system that can be used to present the information and that the visual style and format for the data collected can be developed by the user. The system is illustrated in Fig. 2.1.

The Acquisition of Knowledge Stream

The Acquisition of Knowledge stream is the data collection activity of the modeling system where information in all sense modalities is collected. It is a tracking or documentation of the user's pathway through an educational experience. It is limited to a time frame such as a course, degree, project, or program. The categories of knowledge or data that are to be collected and documented are determined by the user and recorded in this stream. For example, biographical material on artists, artists' writings, and what other people write about an artist become data to be collected in the knowledge base, for example, the record of Paul Klee's theories on visualization. What follows is a historical example of the sources of original data used as the knowledge base in the publication of the Bauhaus teacher and artist Paul Klee's portfolio notebooks. Klee's notebooks combined illustrations, diagrams, and drawings he created in order to describe and document his philosophy of art and his techniques for the teaching of the visual arts at the Bauhaus. The time frame is for a two-year period from 1923 to 1924. The description in Fig. 2.2, by the publisher on the book cover leaf page of the volumes, describes the content of the two-volume work that documents Klee's writings and visual notes. The data collected and reviewed by the editor, Giulio Carlo Argan, are highlighted and are an example of the types of information that an individual may use to develop a database in the knowledge stream:

The following is a transcript of the leaf page of the book cover in the 1973 English edition of the Paul Klee Notebooks, Volume 2, The Nature of Nature, published in the United States by George Witionborn Inc., 1018 Madison Avenue, New York, NY, 10021, 454 pp.

The **writings** which compose Paul Klee's theory of form production and pictorial form have the same importance and the same meaning for modern art as had Leonardo's writings which composed his theory of painting for Renaissance art. Like the latter, they do not constitute a true and proper treatise, that is to say a collection of stylistic and technical rules, but are the result of an introspective analysis which the artist engages in during his work and in the light of the experience of reality which comes to him in the course of his work. This analysis which accompanies and controls the formation of a work of art is a necessary component of the artistic process, the aim and the finality of which are brought to light by it....

So writes Giulio Carlo Argan in his Preface to this first volume of Klee's notebooks. The backbone of his Bauhaus courses was provided by the lecture notes contained in 'Contributions to a Theory of Pictorial Form' which are here published in their entirety. From more than **2,500 pages of the notebooks (consisting of memoranda, teaching projects, constructive drawings,and sketches for his pictures)** it has been possible to reconstruct additional courses of instruction. Also included are the 'Creative Credo', 'Ways of Nature Study,' the Jena lecture 24 and the essay 'Exact Experiments in the Realm of Art.'

The volume includes a magnificent **collection of over one thousand drawings which illustrate the notes**, as well as 188 half-tone illustrations, eight of these reproduced in full color. This second volume of Klee's notebooks follows on where volume one left off, and comprises essentially the notes and illustrations for the 'General system of pictorial media combined with nature study' on which Klee lectured at the Bauhaus in the winter of 1923/4. It overlaps with and complements the material included in volume one, but it is not limited to the lecture notes proper for the years 1923/4. **Related material, problems and notes from Klee's other papers** have also been included where they help to develop particular arguments.

During the period at the Bauhaus covered by the two volumes, Klee was preoccupied in his teaching with the same themes, to which he returned again and again, but the emphasis differed, and in this volume the emphasis is on the study of nature as a starting point for the creative processes of the artist. **The combination of facsimile pages from the artist's lecture notes and drawings and reproductions of the artist's works points up the enormously fertile dialogue between the didactic and introspective side of Klee's career and his own creative output.** In addition to the wealth of formal examples reproduced, the volume includes 243 reproductions of the artist's works, fifteen of them in full color-making a total of over 600 illustrations.

A unique and immensely valuable feature of the English language edition is the **bibliography** by Bernard Karpel of the Museum of Modern Art, New York which has been especially commissioned for this volume. It contains 629 entries of writings by and about the artist.

Reaction Stream

In this stream, users react to knowledge they have acquired. This can be accomplished in one or more sense modalities. The following questions are posed to the user as starting points for reacting to the knowledge base. What are the salient or key ideas of the knowledge base that you the user have been in contact with? What is your reaction to these ideas? Which of them are to be retained or discarded? What are the visual equivalents of the ideas or information? In what sense modalities can they be articulated? In what format can they be articulated? What are your reactions to the knowledge that you have come in contact with? What is your assessment of what you are knowing or learning? These are benchmark questions that contribute to the "constant stream of thought" in which the user records his or her ideas about the knowledge acquired or organized in the reaction stream.

Interpretation and Analysis Zone

An analysis and interpretation of the knowledge you acquire, your previous request for knowledge, and your method for summarizing the knowledge base are contained in the Analysis Interpretation Zone. There are a number of milestones, modes of analysis, and interpretations that are determined by the user to analyze, interpret, judge, and synthesize the requested knowledge. This zone provides the opportunity for the student to engage in critical discourse about the content or knowledge collected and the connections to other disciplines or areas of study. This zone is the documentation students use to know what they have learned. In addition, users define problems and formulate hypotheses of and about the information they have collected (see Fig. 2.1).

Visual Modeling

The modeling activity in this system is the development of visual formats or multimedia formats through which users can illustrate the content and knowledge being documented in each stream. The modeling activity is also important to art students because it is one way of visualizing information in order to explain the data collected in the knowledge stream. Visual modeling should take place in the Acquisition of Knowledge stream, the Interpretation and Analysis Zone, and the Reaction stream where the user is attempting to bring together knowledge streams and show the connections and relationships that may exist between them. Modeling also implies that there is software that can be used to present and organize the data.

Sample Electronic Portfolio Based on the MVMIS

What follows is a sample electronic portfolio created by a student in an art education methods course on the teaching of art history, art criticism, and aesthetics. The assignment was to design and develop a portfolio that would document what they had learned in the course. A paper describing the MVMIS model was presented to the class that stressed the importance of the student taking responsibility for organizing the knowledge stream. Furthermore, the student was required to reflect on and analyze the course content and state their ideas for the teaching of art criticism, art history, and aesthetics. Not every student was required to do an electronic portfolio, so the example in Fig. 2.3 comes from one who chose that option. There was no requirement for use of software. Stefanie Anderson, whose portfolio appears in Fig. 2.3, chose to do it in

Microsoft PowerPoint. The figure is a stroyboard of of Stephanie's presentation, which illustrates how she used the Madeja model to interpret and organize the information.

Fig. 2.3. A Reflective Portfolio by Stephanie Anderson.

Frame 1. Title page of the portfolio.

Frame 2. Identifying a problem presented the course by posing a question.

Fig. 2.3. A Reflective Portfolio by Stephanie Anderson (cont.)

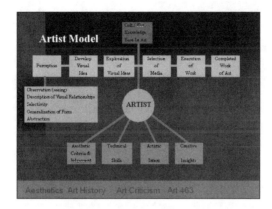

Frame 3. Explaining and Summarizing Knowledge: Interpretation of a model of the artistic process by diagramming and illustrating her conception of artistic model presented and class.

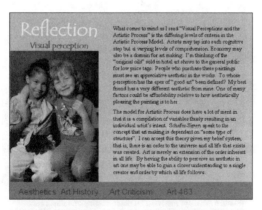

Frame 4. Mode of Analysis: Reflection and analysis of the artist's model and its application to her own idea as to how the artistic process is configured.

Fig. 2.3. A Reflective Portfolio by Stephanie Anderson (cont.)

Frame 5. A transition frame that acts as an introduction to her own model of Art Education using a visual metaphor with text.

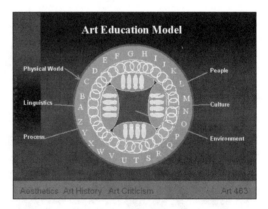

Frame 6. Mode of Analysis: By diagramming and illustrating Stephanie presents an Art Education Model based on her interpretation of the class content. She has organized the content metaphorically by using a circular inter-core surrounded by two concentric circles, which denotes the synergistic quality of her model.

Fig. 2.3. A Reflective Portfolio by Stephanie Anderson (cont.)

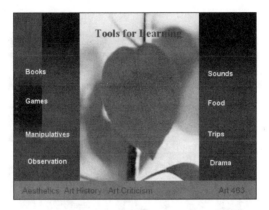

Frame 7. Further visual interpretation of the art education model.

Frame 8. Mode of Analysis: A verbal analysis and interpretation of her art education model using cooking as a verbal metaphor to show how the concepts of her model came together. She emphasizes the importance of aesthetic qualities of experience and art objects in the art program. She also notes the importance of cultural differences in educating the student about art.

Fig. 2.3. A Reflective Portfolio by Stephanie Anderson (cont.)

Frame 9. Introductory frame to cultural aesthetics.

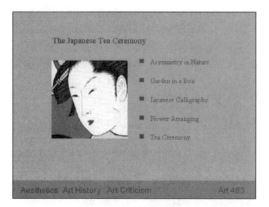

Frame 10. Explaining and Summarizing Knowledge: A data summary of presentations and class discussions on the relationship between the tea ceremony and the aesthetics of Japanese art and culture.

Fig. 2.3. A Reflective Portfolio by Stephanie Anderson (cont.)

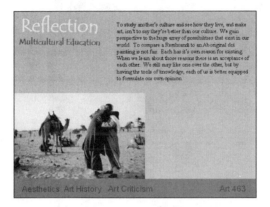

Frame 11. Reaction Stream: Reaction and reflection about the relationship of multicultural education to aesthetics and the visual arts. This is an example of using the content or data presented in class about the Japanese tea ceremony and the concepts listed in the previous frame and relating them to the teaching of the art.

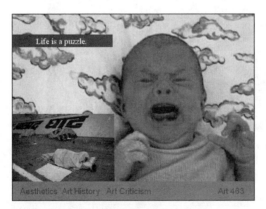

Frame 12. This frame is the segue to move from cultural aesthetics to aesthetics in the popular culture and the natural and constructed environment.

Fig. 2.3. A Reflective Portfolio by Stephanie Anderson (cont.)

Frame 13. Explaining and Summarizing Knowledge: This is a summary of Stephanie's examples of aesthetic puzzles and contradictions that exist in the world around us.

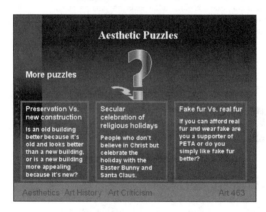

Frame 14. Continuation of Frame 13.

Fig. 2.3. A Reflective Portfolio by Stephanie Anderson (cont.)

Frame 15. Mode of Analysis: Stephanie's discussion of aesthetic puzzles in the human experience.

Frame 16. This frame is the segue to move from aesthetics puzzles to art criticism.

Fig. 2.3. A Reflective Portfolio by Stephanie Anderson (cont.)

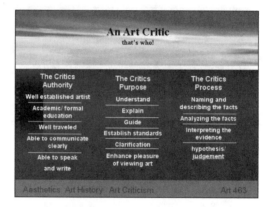

Frame 17. Explaining and Summarizing Knowledge: By diagramming and illustrating, Stephanie presents her interpretation of the class content on the critic.

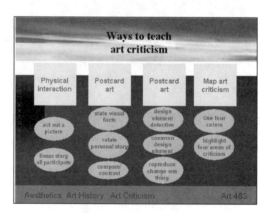

Frame 18. Reaction Stream: Reaction and reflection about the relationship of art criticism to aesthetics and the visual arts, and an example of using the content or data presented in class and relating them to the teaching of art.

Fig. 2.3. A Reflective Portfolio by Stephanie Anderson (cont.)

Frame 19. Continuation of Frame 18.

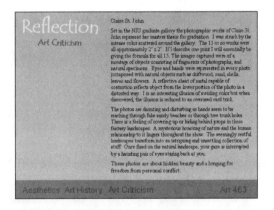

Frame 20. Mode of Analysis: Stephanies' analysis of critical inquiry as it relates to the works of art in the student's world.

Fig. 2.3. A Reflective Portfolio by Stephanie Anderson (cont.)

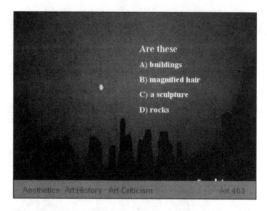

Frame 21 and Frame 22. This frame is the segue to move from art criticism to metaphorming.

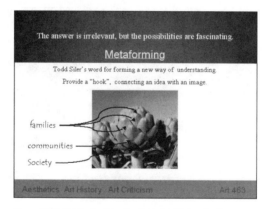

Frame 22. Explaining and Summarizing Knowledge: By diagramming and illustrating, Stephanie presents her interpretation of the class content on metaphorming as defined by Tod Siler.

Fig. 2.3. A Reflective Portfolio by Stephanie Anderson (cont.)

Frame 23. Reaction Stream: Reaction and reflection about the relationship of art and aesthetics to metaphor as defined by Tod Siler.

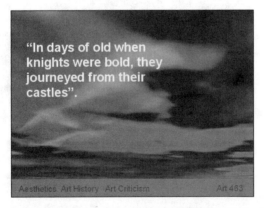

Frame 24. This frame is the segue to move from metaphorming to art history.

Fig. 2.3. A Reflective Portfolio by Stephanie Anderson (cont.)

Frame 25. Explaining and Summarizing Knowledge: By diagramming and illustrating Stephanie presents her interpretation of the class content on art history..

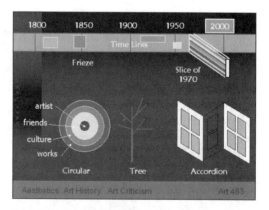

Frame 26. Continuation of Frame 25.

Study Questions

1. Find historical examples of the folios of artists, designers, and scholars exemplifying the Modeling of Visual Information such as DaVinci's Codex Madrid I and II, Christo, and Jean-Claude documentation of their projects such as Umbrellas or Charles Darwin's The Origins of the Species (1859). Identify strategies, formats, and categories of information collected that illustrates the visual modeling of information and how visualization can explain information.
2. Assessments and mass testing are becoming a public issue. Survey the web, national and local newspapers, and magazines for articles that address evaluation issues in our schools and universities. Write a short essay about the politics of standardized testing and schooling in the United States.
3. Create a panel made up of students and assign issues related to assessment of expressive activities discussed in this chapter, such as the relationship between the curriculum and standardized testing, the politics of national and state testing in our schools, and public reaction to mass testing programs.

References

Askin, W. (1985). *Evaluating the advanced placement portfolio in studio art* (Advanced Placement Program Monograph). NJ: Educational Testing Service.
Darwin, Charles. (1979). *The Origin of the Species.* New York: Random House, a replication of original manuscript.
Davis, D. J., Thuernau, P. K., Hudgens, A., & Hall, B. W. (1971–1973). *Final report: The arts in general education project evaluation component.* St. Louis, MO: CEMREL.
Hall, B., & Thuernau, P. (1975). *Formative evaluation in the aesthetic education program* (Bulletin No. 43, Summer). Council for Research in Music Education, School of Music, University of Illinois, Urbana, IL.
Kintner, M. (1933). *Measurement of artistic abilities.* Carnegie Foundation, Psychological Corporation.New York, NY
Madeja, S. S. (1959). *A survey of existing art measurement devices.* Unpublished masters thesis, University of Minnesota, Minneapolis, MN.
Madeja, S. S. (Ed.). (1978). *Structuring a research agenda for the arts and aesthetics, first-year book on research and arts and aesthetic education, arts and aesthetics: An agenda for the future.* St. Louis, MO: CEMREL.
Madeja, S. S. (2002). Statement from the transcript of an unpublished interview.
Madeja, S. S., & Onuska, S. (1977). *Through the arts to the aesthetic.* St. Louis, MO: CEMREL.
Reti, L (Ed). (1974) *The unkown Leonardo.* New York, NY: McGraw-Hill
Smith, L. M., & Geoffrey, W. (1968). *The complexities of an urban classroom.* New York: Holt, Rinehart, & Winston.

THE CHARACTER OF EXPRESSIVE LEARNING AND ITS ASSESSMENT

The school assessment context as presented in chapter 1 raises a number of questions regarding the role of the teacher in the assessment process, including what kinds of assessments art teachers use versus those used by students and artists, teachers' lack of assessment training, and the appropriateness of paper-and-pencil, true-false, or multiple-choice tests in assessing student progress. Chapter 2 identified several alternatives to paper-and-pencil tests in art, including different approaches to portfolio assessment, and considered the connections between assessment and the school curriculum. This chapter examines the utility of authentic assessment as a way to involve art teachers as stakeholders in the assessment process and provides reasons for the project using an authentic approach to student portfolio assessment.

The Pressures for Reform

Although school reformers see testing as a significant part of reform, very little effort has been expended on determining how such testing relates to what teachers teach. Cusic (1994) observed that stakeholders in school reform should accept that teachers' personal interpretation and choice are central to their professionalism. If not wholly autonomous, teachers operate in their classrooms in an independent and self-reliant manner. They usually behave as individuals and not as a collective force. Yet most often teachers do not feel free to join or not to join the reform effort; they are subject to state-mandated compliance. Cusic argued that, if teachers are the deciding element in school reform, they should be able to decide whether to join the reform effort and, furthermore, be able to regulate themselves and set their own policies and their own standards. In Cusic's view, however, regulators and reformers fear that granting such freedom will cause teachers to question the reforms and even argue for increased individual rights and privileges; they will not reform their teaching and, therefore, learning will not improve. Given a choice, reformers of this mind-set would rather mandate teacher compliance and, eventually, also mandate the means for assessment.

The Art Teacher's Role in Reform

For effective art education, we do need to know what our students are learning, but, as Eisner (1992) noted, no one has yet answered the question of why some reformers believe they can embarrass teachers and school administrators into higher levels of professional performance through the imposition of a single set of predetermined educational standards. Is there any reason, Eisner asked, why we should expect new educational policy reforms to have any greater influence than those of the past? Will better teaching and more caring schools be created by a national report card that forces every student to arrive at the same destination at the same time, with a single set of aims, curriculum, and standards for all?

Such reforms can make teachers more cynical and more passive, principally because they have seen so many bandwagons come and go.

Education, Eisner (1992) wrote, is: about learning to deal with uncertainty and ambiguity. It is about learning how to savor the quality of the journey. It is about becoming critically minded, intellectually curious and learning how to frame and pursue your own education aims. It is not about regaining our competitive edge. (p. 2)

Like Eisner, most people working in schools doubt that federal initiatives for standardization will make a difference; they believe that change must come from within, rather than from outside, the schools. Arts educators can contribute to this change process, but only if they accept the empowerment will they become the principal change agents in educational decision making.

However, even if one believes in Eisner's (1992) ideal education, the testing and assessment of student progress are matters of importance in the school community, demanding answers as to whether art learnings are assessable and, if so, what learnings need to be assessed.

What We Need to Assess

Although the federal and most state governments are currently committed to testing all elementary and secondary students, no standardized visual arts tests other than the National Assessment of Educational Progress (NAEP) model are available. Also, paper-and-pencil, true-false, and multiple-choice tests, and even essay questions, rarely provide adequate estimates of what students learn in most K–12 school art programs, where studio-based activity is the primary means of instruction. What the national reform effort most obviously lacks is any single art test that can measure what students know and are able to do in all of the nation's art programs. The reasons that no such tests are available are the lack of adequate means to quantify expressive activity and the unwillingness of all the nation's art teachers to teach art in the same way.

Art Learning as Part of the Total Curriculum

Many educators today believe that creative performances in art are just another form of critical thinking, but as D. N. Perkins (1990) noted, critical thinking is only part of creative thinking. Whereas the outcome of creative thinking is primarily creation, the outcome of critical thinking is a sound assessment of things. Sometimes the two outcomes meld into one, but generally the overlap between the objectives of creative and critical thinking is modest, because critical assessments often and unproblematically fail the creativity's originality criterion. A good assessment of a play, a business plan, or a holiday spot may be, but does not need to be, particularly original. Emphasis falls on the assessment's soundness, not on its originality. Likewise, a creative outcome may happen to be, but is not typically, an assessment.

Combining Critical and Creative Modes of Thought

Perkins (1990) raised a number of important questions, some of which have already been posed by arts educators concerned about discipline-based art education (DBAE) approaches. He asked whether (a) an individual's creativity depends on particular content mastery, (b) too much knowledge inhibits creativity, or (c) students might overmaster a domain and become trapped by a repertoire of reflexive beliefs and procedures. While observing that productivity may depend on mastery of a particular content, Perkins also noted that too much knowledge may inhibit creativity and that thinking skills do not transfer beyond the context of learning unless instruction directly addresses the problems of transfer and encourages students to monitor their own use of a skill and apply it. Students who do not internalize a strategy because they are given insufficient practice, he wrote, also feel uncomfortable with the skill and as a consequence do not use it. In Perkins' thoughts, it may again be time to bring critical thinking and performing into a single focus, especially in the arts where educators who think creatively know better than anyone else how to reflect on their own endeavors.

Although empirical studies have generally not confirmed J. P. Guilford's (1967) so-called fluency, flexibility, and remote associates modes, Perkins (1990) identified several attributes of creative thinking that suggest it is essential to students' general education. These include problem-finding patterns of thinking—the connections between creative thinking, valuing, and intrinsic motivation—as identified by Jacob Getzels and Mihaly Csikszentmihalyi (1976).

Problem-finding behaviors suggest that creative thinkers search more extensively for problems worth solving and show greater flexibility in defining problems. Getzels and Csikszentmihalyi (1976) found that student artists invested much more time than others did in exploring what sort of work to attempt, remained ready to change directions, and, when alternatives were suggested by the work in progress, were more willing to alter their behavior. They also found that problem-finder students, faced with the setup of a still life, would explore many possibilities, set aside some objects, and bring back others before deciding what arrangement was best. Creative patterns of thinking, which Perkins (1990) defined as "thinking frames," are evident when individuals decide on a direction or pursue a change in direction.

The connections between creative thinking and values, especially a person's commitments and aspirations, have been well documented in the literature by Frank Barron (1969). Creative artists and scientists both appear to have a high tolerance for ambiguity, disorganization, and asymmetry. Creative people appear to enjoy the challenge of dealing with ambiguity and with forging new unities.

More important, creative values seem to inspire intrinsic motivation, defined by Perkins (1990) as valuing something for its own sake. Psychologist Teresa Amabile

(1983) found that people tend to function most creatively on those endeavors where they feel high intrinsic motivation. Other studies suggest that creative scientists feel a deep-seated investment in their work, and studies by Barron (1972) suggest that artists and poets show extreme dedication to their craft. These studies also suggest not only that creative people enjoy originality and ambiguity, but that such behaviors actually are the causes of creativity, which is to say that people are more or less creative because of the values they embrace. This means, according to Perkins (1990), that conspicuous creativity emerges because the person is trying to be creative, that is, is intentionally producing original and appropriate things because he or she values the behavior.

Arts educators believe that creative values can be taught directly or encouraged in arts classes and therefore focus on the forms of thought the arts best teach. As previously noted, these creative thinking skills do not transfer well unless students have sufficient practice to internalize them and are guided toward opportunities to use them. This suggests, in addition, that educators need to seek ways to link creative thought to creative (artistic) behavior.

Creative Thinking and Creative Performing

To promote creative thinking, arts educators link it to what the arts do best: make new things. Sam Hope (1991) believes that K–12 education encompasses three basic intellectual functions: finding out how existing things work, producing new or unique things, and finding out what has happened. The science function is centered on discovering how things work, the history function on what happened, and the art function on making new things. Hope sees these intellectual functions applied in all disciplines but with different priorities and sequences. For example, whereas science-based enterprise has interest in what happened and in creating new things, it is primarily interested in how the natural world works. History-based enterprise is also concerned with how things work, but through understanding what happened. Finally, arts-based enterprise is concerned with how things work, but as accomplished in creating new things.

Hope (1991) argued further that, because contemporary society is characterized by an information and knowledge explosion, schools need not only to teach students to use their minds, but also to introduce the life of the mind: Serious work in the arts disciplines, he holds, exemplifies the life of the mind because works of art represent some of humanity's greatest achievements; its methods provide means for both knowing and apprehending the world, involve the crafting of integrated solutions to specific problems, and create products meant for discourse.

Hope's (1991) three major intellectual enterprises can be viewed as the philosophical frames of mind that shape logical thought. The historical frame uses a deductive approach to understanding by matching objects and events with prior assumptions, the scientific frame uses induction to study events and objects over time, and the artistic frame uses practical arguments in both the inductive and deductive modes toward making creative products. Hope believes that schools emphasize the results of scientific, historical, and artistic efforts rather than focus on the modes of inquiry themselves. The study of all three modes is important, but for an arts-centered education, we must use artistic modes of inquiry that stress (a) strong technical competence in creating and recreating art, based on an understanding of how art disciplines work and have worked in the past; (b) a thorough understanding of the elements to be employed, not only how the elements work and their past uses, but also possible new uses; and (c) the ability to discern contexts and conditions that surround the making and reception of a specific work.

Discovering Alternative Modes of Thought

Hope's (1991) intellectual enterprises, which link artistic thinking and making by taking what a student knows and applying it successfully in aesthetic circumstances, are very similar to the philosophical perspective on critical and reflective thinking advanced by Richard Paul (1990). Paul outlined what he called a philosophy-based approach to teaching critical thinking across the curriculum and proposed that it could transform classroom instruction and activities. Like Hope, Paul believes that critical and reflective thinking can be improved by using philosophy as a field of study, as a mode of thinking, and as a framework for thinking.

For Paul (1990), a philosophical approach is most appropriate for an educational setting because it is (a) individualistic, in that participants do not agree except broadly; (b) a means of critical discussion, rational cross-examination, and dialectical exchange; and (c) a metacognitive mode forming a framework for thought about thinking. Science, he believes, limits the range of issues to consider, is too deterministic, and fails to offer a variety of ways for analyzing human lives and for living them. In virtually all cases no person can validate answers to philosophical questions for another. Paul also believes that the unphilosophical mind thinks without a clear sense of the foundations of its own thought and of the most basic concepts, aims, assumptions, and values that define and direct that thought. In other words, the unphilosophical mind is unaware that it thinks within a system, within a framework, or within a philosophy:

> The philosophical mind gives serious considerations to alternative and competing concepts, aims, assumptions, and values, enters empathetically into thinking fundamentally different from its own, and does not confuse its thinking with reality. By habitually thinking in a global way, the philosophical mind gains foundational self-command,and is comfortable when problems cross disciplines, domains, and frameworks. (Paul, p. 448)

Therefore, to assess arts education programs that will open children to alternative modes of thinking (which are the forms of thinking the arts do best) and will develop in children a life of the mind, we must pursue an assessment policy that takes into account critical thinking, philosophical thinking, and creative performing. Also critically important is beginning with the education of arts teachers.

Because we need to link the processes of thinking and making, critical thinking in the arts must be linked to creative practice. In doing so, it is necessary for the arts program to provide philosophically coherent strategies to integrate historical, scientific, and aesthetic enterprises so that thinking and making cohere. This requires that our teaching paradigms reflect the frames of thought that students and teachers can use to think about and to make art and that the paradigms also, in a synergistic and integrative way, bring artistic thinking and making into a single construct—one that is both cross-disciplinary and responsive to critical thought.

A student's artwork evolves through an intuitive encounter with the visual elements generated in the work. These elements incorporate Bell's (1958) view on art structure, Langer's (1953) on pure appearances, Dewey's (1934) on personal growth, and Heidegger's (1971) on personal form: All four accept as paramount both the artist's private vision and the art object. The form or gestalt concept in the visual arts includes all approaches that center on the artist's using the marks generated in making as a means for achieving an intuitively objectified form or gestalt. In this aesthetic, the art form has a life of its own, one uniquely formed through the artist's intuitive feelings, and it is understood in terms of the viewer's experience with such feeling states.

The gestalt paradigm in the studio is based on the student's self-knowledge and the intuitive responses generated in the act of forming in materials. The study of art history in this paradigm involves understanding how the artist's individually articulated feelings are conveyed in the work's divergent forms and patterns. Aesthetically, art is significant form, containing feelings articulated and uniquely understood by both the artist and the viewer, but with no direct effort to communicate.

If general educational reform is to be successful, it must go beyond requiring all students to learn the same things in the same way according to the same timetable. The arts provide the alternative modes of thinking that students need; they are best equipped to teach and encourage learning that philosophically connects thinking and making. School reform in art, therefore, should be in the hands of the arts teachers, rather than being imposed as a top-down assessment designed to embarrass them into developing a single curriculum with a single set of aims and standards for all.

The Quantification of Qualitative Learning

The principal question this project sought to answer was whether the aesthetic object can be assessed quantitatively. The issue will always remain debatable among aestheticians and artists, many of whom argue that expressive objects are more the result of a state of mind than objective fact. Aestheticians like Robin Collingwood would claim that art cannot even be evaluated, because one cannot know what an object will be in advance of its making. Creative artists in general believe that art is a product of intuition and inspiration and that, even if the art object is deemed useful or functional, that practicality is not what makes it art.

Art teachers in public education, although agreeing with the artists' creative point of view, also know that in schooling, products of instruction that cannot be evaluated are products that to all intents and purposes do not exist. The choice for teachers is to either find a way to assess arts instruction or witness its eventual elimination from the school curriculum. The most popular political choice today is to assess art for its utility in solving a variety of school problems: keeping kids in schools, improving academic performance and graduation rates, and helping diminish juvenile crime and drug abuse. Using the arts as an alibi for the pursuit of other objectives raises a haunting question: Will proving that art can do what every other subject in the curriculum can do only further assure its redundancy in an overcrowded and underfunded school curriculum?

To answer the quantification question, however, we must first know how we know that what our students are learning has sufficient subject validity for us to conclude that the art curriculum provides for an accurate and sufficient representation of both the means and products of artistic inquiry. We most need to know whether the learning—what we want students to know and do—is linked to art's methods and products. Epistemologically, this is to assure us that what students learn in art classrooms is related to art itself.

Art Learning

In achieving an aesthetically testable object, it is necessary first to decide what the nature of the art object is. In Kantian terms, art exists where the self is both subject and object, where context has to do with how objects and the self are shaped in an aesthetic process that inseparably joins form, matter, making, and meaning. Put more specifically, this viewpoint argues that, when the self is both subject and object, growth in aesthetic capability requires engagement with aesthetic objects or events: engagement that contributes to the knowledge of self, that requires qualitative rather than quantitative knowledge of the objects and the self, and whose cultural meanings are shaped by individual and private experiences with aesthetic objects.

When an aesthetic context exists, it involves human experiences that shape both object and self, with aesthetic capabilities being increased through events that shape both the maker and the thing made, the observer and the thing observed; where contact with the artist's work makes artists out of all who are involved in aesthetic encounters; and where some works are judged to be more worthwhile than others. That definition also suggests that it may be impossible to distinguish between the maker and the thing made, which puts the making of an object in a Deweyinian sense both something the maker does and something he or she mentally undergoes. That duality requires that we define the aesthetic object through those actions of the learner that create new products and those that create new ways of thinking and behaving; those actions are, in essence, what arts students do when engaged in expressive forming. What this requires, in order for us to know what the student knows, is the adoption of an evaluation process concerned with assessing the processes of thinking and making as manifested in the products and also assessing methods of inquiry required for learning in the arts.

Art Learning Standards

Although useful in setting curriculum standards, National Goals 2000 (1994) and the National Standards, Music Educators National Conference (MENC) (1994) were also designed to encourage knowledge transferability among disciplines, promote cultural diversity and appropriate technologies, and serve as a foundation for student assessment. Arts standards are nevertheless an important assessment tool, as they do reveal those standards the arts disciplines seem to agree on and also those on which they do not. On the positive side, they provide us with a generic language fitting all the disciplines that enables us to talk about assessment objectives; on the negative side, they do so in a language disconnected with the creative act and, consequently, with epistemology (what most arts teachers are trying to teach and most arts learners are actually learning).

To those experienced in the art of creating multidisciplinary curriculum standards, especially where the task is to unite several different disciplinary perspectives, it is evident that whatever language one decides on that is not objectionable to those in a number of different disciplines also ends up not having much relevance to any discipline. One only needs to analyze the national content standards in the four arts disciplines to see also that, although the standards differ in number and the kinds of tasks performed, each discipline can ultimately be reduced to five essential artworld content domains: (a) performing and making, (b) organizing and structuring, (c) criticizing, (d) historical and cultural knowing, and (e) relatedness to other disciplines.

This model for a unified approach to describing arts content first appeared in the College Board's Project Equality, which was at the time clearly influenced by psychologist Jerome Bruner's (1960) notion that, to educate a student in physics (art), it was necessary to educate him or her as a physicist (artist) and by Manuel Barkan's (1962) notion that to be fully educated in art one should study art production, art history, and art criticism.

Art Practice

To develop standards that are aesthetic and testable requires that we move beyond merely claiming that art learning is creative, intuitive, and expressive to actually identifying the behaviors involved in high-quality artistic performing and thinking. One very useful approach to that identification and the one used in the construction of the study instruments is found in the work of Vernon Howard (1977), who provided some conceptions of artistic practice, noting both what practice is and what it is not. Practice in action, he believes, involves repeating an action guided by specific aims in order to solve various kinds of problems and to build skills and abilities. To practice an action is to repeat it with the aim of improving it and eventually mastering it. That process may range in complexity from the mere elimination of errors to capturing the proper mood of an expressive form. Practice is not, in his view, the mere repetition of exercises until the performer "gets it right" and can do it without thought. The cognitive aim of practice is, rather, to achieve knowledge not only of the fact that one has succeeded or failed to perform at a given level, but also of why this is the case. To incorporate practice as part of teaching, Howard believes it is far more important to have a clear concept of the practice and what is to be accomplished by it than to understand "mastery" or "greatness," except to the degree that this understanding gives direction to practice itself.

Students Needing to Know That and How to Do That

Howard (1977) views awareness as a significant part of a conceptual topology of practice that includes the role of knowledge, awareness, and routinization. Here, he divides the issue into two major parts, forming the strategic distinctions between types of awareness involved in (a) the routinization of behavior and (b) epistemological sorting of ordinary practice concepts, including habits, faculties, and skills. The epistemological component includes traditional concerns for propositional knowledge, that is, distinguishing knowing that from procedural knowledge, which is to know how. Here, he notes that traditional historical, critical, philosophical, or psychological study of the arts takes the form of propositional knowledge about art and performance competencies are considered those involved with procedural know-how. Procedural knowledge, to Howard, includes skill acquisition, routinization, and the development of skills that may involve, but cannot be reduced to, propositional judgment. Knowing how to do something propositionally, he argued, is neither necessary nor sufficient to one's knowing how to accomplish the task itself, where propositional knowledge is limited to standards of belief, truth, and evidence, and procedural knowledge is the result of repeated trials as well as newly discovered standards of achievement. Thus, for Howard, awareness is both cognizance of the circumstances necessary for determining the needed behavior and also cognizance of what occurs in carrying out that behavior; the first is a symbol-based awareness and the other a behavior-based awareness. He considers both necessary for a skill's routinization, which in turn becomes a process both of ceasing to be propositionally aware and of becoming newly aware of a relevant bit of know-how. Much of what we know, he argued, never crosses the threshold of awareness, yet controlled improvement suggests some things are brought to awareness and some are suppressed in the efforts of efficiency.

In art practice, Howard (1977) believes that a focal and a peripheral awareness are equally and highly relevant, which means to be aware of what one is doing, to be able to describe it, and to explain one's actions in a detached, scientific manner. This aspect of knowing he calls knowing what to think about, that is, what precepts, images, or sensations to keep in consciousness at any stage of a skilled performance. Using a nailing activity as a metaphor, he pointed out that when we drive the nail we pay attention to both the nail and the hammer, but in different ways. We watch the effect of our strokes on the nail, and we also wield the hammer so as to hit the nail squarely. This means being physically aware of the sensations associated with the hammering, as well as being focally aware of driving a nail.

For Howard (1977), the artistic problem is, then, to know both how and what, which is to make a distinction between knowing what something is and knowing the experiencing of it. Here, he notes that knowing that something is red is not the same as seeing red; knowing that an object in a painting can be seen as appearing from either above or below is something one cannot actually see until one actually does it or experiences it for oneself. This is, in his view, the distinction between knowing what it is to do something and knowing what it is like to do it. Propositional knowing, that is, what to think about (focally), is therefore different from knowing what it is to perform properly, in spite of one's effort to do everything one has been taught to do.

Howard's (1977) argument clearly demonstrates that knowing something propositionally is fundamentally different from knowing the use of that knowledge in practice; to realize this is to grasp the distinction between knowing what something is and knowing what it is to experience something. Hence, a knowledge about art is a distinctly different kind of knowing from the kind of knowing associated with the actual making of artistic objects. More importantly, he argued, improvement in what is accomplished in the act of practice suggests an increased knowledge of what one wants to accomplish and a transference of focal to procedural knowledge. What this transfer suggests in an assessment sense is that any effort to assess artistic practice must address both the student's focal and procedural knowledge.

Students Learning to Know What

Focal or propositional forms of knowing in art require students to know (a) what they are doing and to be able to describe it and explain that action; (b) what to think about and what precepts, images, and sensations to keep in consciousness in the process of practice; (c) what concept is to be practiced; (d) what caused a failure to perform; (e) what they need to be good at; and (f) what historical, cultural, and philosophical knowledge is necessary. To be successful in art, a student clearly must have a broad range of historical, critical, aesthetic, and technical knowledge about art. These knowledges permit, in Howard's (1977) topology, the other forms of knowing listed previously. One cannot function effectively in art if one does not have such historical, critical, technical, or aesthetic knowledge. Yet these knowledges are useful only in the context of a problem to be solved; they are useful in knowing what kind of critical thinking is necessary to solve that problem. All forms of knowledge about art are, therefore, useful, but in art practice, they are useful only as they affect the procedural knowledges necessary for active forming.

Students Learning to Know How

Procedural forms of knowing in art require that a student:
• Know how to create something.
• Have the skills to accomplish tasks.

- Know his or her standard of achievement.
- Know what occurs in the creative process.
- Know what it is to experience something.

Procedural knowledge in artistic conception is, in Howard's (1977) view, the result of creative activity and is also the consequence of and emerges from the activity itself. It includes knowing what it is to know how to create, having command of the skills necessary to do it, recognizing when it has been done effectively, and knowing how one got to that point through an experiential process. As a process, it has to do with both correcting errors and establishing a mode of thought, which is to make the creative act itself a state of expressive consciousness.

Procedural knowledge is also, as Howard suggested, an awareness of the circumstances and the behaviors needed to create: the elimination of propositional awareness in the interest of knowing how to accomplish something, what to think about when doing it, and what precepts, images, or sensations to keep in consciousness at any stage of the creative act. Procedural knowledge is, thus, also technical knowledge, which means students need to master skills and techniques in order to make expression possible and to create images available to vision. Visual concepts that require the integration of images and abstract forms cannot be realized without possessing the skills and techniques necessary to construct a visual concept that will allow us not only to see what we have imagined, but also to evaluate its effectiveness. Without art skills and techniques, the student cannot effectively carry out the actions required to develop a visual image, nor can the student integrate into that concept the focal knowledge, emotion, ideas, and creative inspiration essential to the evolution of expressive form. Artistic skill seems irrelevant to those who do not make art, but even those artists who deny that skill is important really do know that, without skills, they would lack the power to create and would also lack self-confidence, flexibility in visual problem solving, and even the understanding of art itself. As Howard (1977) notes, the maker must know how to create, possess the skills to do it, know whether a goal has been reached, know what is occurring in the process, and know what it is to experience that process.

Assessing Expressive Learning

To assess both the products and the methods of artistic inquiry, one must also go beyond the construction of paper-and-pencil, true-false, and multiple-choice forms of testing, seeking instead alternative forms of assessment that focus on evaluating the individual and the products of expressive inquiry. In current test jargon, such efforts are referred to as authentic assessment.

An assessment is authentic when it involves students in tasks that are worthwhile, significant, and meaningful. Such assessments will appear as learning activities, involve conceptual and higher order thinking skills, and interrelate several different forms of knowledge. They make explicit the basis for judging the students' work and are, in effect, standard setting rather than standard testing in character.

Authentic assessment thus makes the development of the student's content and achievement standards the ultimate goal in the instructional program.

The philosophy of every authentic assessment should reflect three conditions:
1. All statements about assessment should look back to the purpose or artistic intent of the activity.
2. Assessment is not the pursuit of a perfect scoring guide or perfect documentation.
3. The assessment plan should center on the student's development of the artistic intent, expression, and skill that make creative vision possible.

Setting Assessment Objectives

A school-based, authentic art assessment program should include assessments that:

- Can be used to evaluate student arts performances at every level of the school art program.

- Recognize that students have diverse backgrounds, abilities, and learning styles and that make explicit the standards for judging the work.

- Use grading processes that reflect performance goals and reveal student and program strengths rather than weaknesses.

- Can be scored according to clearly stated performance objectives.

Making the assessment authentic also involves understanding that efforts need to be focused on helping students learn. We need to be clear about what we want students to know and be able to do. We also need to be sure that the measures we use and the results we obtain accurately reflect what the students do really know and are able to do. In authentic assessment we must keep in mind that our goals are to improve the quality of student learning and to capitalize on the students' strengths rather than on their weaknesses. The bottom line in authentic assessment is really about helping students set their own high standards of achievement.

Knowing What Performances to Assess

It is through knowing what we want students to know and be able to do that we can determine the skills and knowledges critical to students' expressive development and also decide the performance measures most likely to assess their skills and knowledge at a given level. In general, the performances we need to assess are: (a) the expressive quality of the students' work, (b) the knowledge base from which their aesthetic judgments are formed, and (c) how they advance in their conceptual development.

Assessing Expressive Performances

To assess the expressive development in students' creative work, a number of holistic instruments need to be developed in order to answer the question of whether the instructional program and the students' learning are philosophically consistent with the means and ends of art. An additional question is whether the curriculum has sufficient subject validity to provide for accurate and significant representation of the products of artistic inquiry as well as the means for that inquiry. Holistic assessments that objectify expressive knowledge will increase as the students' expressive efforts increase in their purposefulness and intensity. As students advance from K–12, the number and variety of such assessments should increase in both the focal and procedural knowledges assessed and in the degree of integration achieved between the ends and means of expression.

Assessing Program Knowledge and Skills

Student products may not always reveal the specific knowledges and skills used in their production. However, for instructional purposes we need to know how successful we are in providing such knowledge and how valuable the knowledge is in achieving expressive kinds of knowing. Thus, some analytic measures are also needed for assessing an art program. Furthermore, because students learn differently and require different kinds of knowledge for success, these analytic assessments need a scope and variety sufficient to assess a broad range of instructional circumstances and grade levels. At times, a checklist instrument is appropriate to indicate the absence or presence of a given knowledge, skill, or ability; a checklist is especially useful in the early years of schooling when teachers face larger numbers of students and lower order cognitive abilities. As students mature expressively and cognitively, the use of analytic measures to assess student creative work should be more frequent and should concentrate on focal and procedural knowledge. Knowledge and skill assessments are used to estimate the curriculum's psychological validity, which takes into account human growth and development, learning, individual differences, and the like. For diagnostic purposes, analytic assessments answer the questions of what can be taught, when and to whom, as well as the art program's effectiveness in achieving general education goals and the particular knowledges and skills associated with study in art history, art structure, and art evaluation.

Assessing Conceptual Development

Because concept formation in art is neither solely a matter of development nor always evidenced in individual creative works, teachers should also holistically assess a selected body of student work over time. This assessment can uncover the changes occurring in the student's thinking and whether the student's visual concepts are becoming more complex and better integrated, for example, exhibiting more extensive and intensive knowledge, wider integrations, more precise perceptual differentiations, and increasingly more perceptual evidence. We may also want to know about the student's use of inductive, deductive, and heuristic logic and the student's progress in the ability to analyze, compare, construct, reorder, adapt, stimulate, test, and synthesize various ideas, values, and images.

Evidence of such integrations is most likely to be found in a student portfolio that includes samples of student work collected by the teacher over several months or a semester. The work should be assessed in the order of its creation and should also, if possible, be supported by student self-evaluations addressing particular forms of integration, which would then be a supplementary record of the student's cognitive growth over time. The teacher should look at the portfolio holistically, recording observations in a log book that could then be used to support a particular observation or to observe trends or consistencies.

Making Assessment Manageable

No one art teacher in any one school is capable of assessing all of his or her students' art achievement. For the elementary art specialist with 1,300 children and nine classes per day, about all one can expect is some effort at a checklist documentation and a gestalt look at the children's development as they progress in that teacher's class over the years. For those teaching in middle school, some effort at analytic assessment is quite feasible and, for those at the high school level with more advanced portfolio classes, a more holistic look at a student's progress over time is not only possible but critical. If a school district is truly concerned with doing an authentic assessment, however, it should release teachers from some of their regular classroom responsibilities. Time is needed to meet various assessment tasks, provide for some division of labor in developing and using the assessment tools, and, in general, facilitate a cooperative effort among the art teachers in a school or within the district. The Vermont Assessment Project (VAAP, 1995) suggested four ways for doing this: (a) spreading the assessment among grade levels, (b) spreading the assessment across teachers, (c) spreading the assessment across expertise, and (d) targeting certain grade levels for assessment

The Development of Test Instruments

Developing a test instrument requires consideration of a number of important factors about American art instruction, including that: (a) the goals are diverse, (b) making and performing remain the dominant modes of instruction, (c) students reflect divergent learning styles, (d) varied problem finding and solving are desired behaviors, and (e) evidence of achievement occurs mainly in products that meld both focal and procedural knowledge.

The Art Teacher's Involvement in Assessment

Although most art teachers know they need to assess instruction, they also have difficulty deciding what they need to teach and in what order. The reason is, in part, the range and variety of content material they are expected to cover and the kinds of learning environments in which many work. When teachers are expected to teach studio production as well as the understanding of art and culture, relate these to other forms of knowledge, critically assess and evaluate works of art, and make connections between all of this and the real world, they simply have far too much to do. This is especially so if they are teaching nine 25-minute periods a day to over 1,300 children a week. Not all art teachers, of course, face such odds; however, many do, especially at the elementary level. Even if they could accomplish everything, they still would have to meet the additional responsibilities of helping students improve in their other academic subjects, stay in school, remain drug free, graduate, and so forth. This over burdening suggests that we need to focus first on what we want students to be able to do and second on the kinds of student performances that provide the richest content and the greatest utility in a given classroom.

Assessing What Art Teachers Teach

When we anchor instructional outcomes to what teachers teach and students learn, we achieve three advantages over top-down reforms driven by administrative fiat. First, the teacher has ownership of both the learning and the evaluation process; second, the teacher is responsible for making his or her goals clear to the student and to the school; and third, the assessment process is fair to all parties: the student, the teacher, and the school.

Moreover, when we link assessment directly to what is taught, teachers no longer feel required to perform according to someone else's rules, but rather according to their own teaching goals: The responsibility is placed squarely on the teacher, who must ensure that the instruction matches the goals and that the results clearly reflect the goals. To do this in an ill-defined domain requires that student learning in art production, art history, and art criticism be evident in the written, spoken, and visual products of instruction in both the expressive and cognitive domains.

Art teachers really have the greatest stake in what they want students to learn. When assessment is linked to instruction itself, teachers provide the reasons by which others should measure significant learning. Who is better qualified than the art teacher to set standards?

The Art Learning Environment

Choosing modes of assessment consistent with art learning requires recognizing the character of sound art curriculum. Learning activity: (a) is directed toward outcomes, (b) addresses two or more objectives concurrently, (c) affords opportunities for varied and multiple responses, and (d) allows students to take ownership of their own learning. Assessing modes consistent with art must take into account that the learning is sequential, that knowledges are transferable from art to other disciplines, and that artistic learning involves perception, technical practice, mastery, and creative expression. All these concerns provide what Fraenkel called a well-structured learning environment (Slavick, 1995).

Learning Through Doing

Art teachers in most school art programs focus on the practical activity of making expressive objects. Effective art teachers use visual exemplars, teach about the principles of design and the plastic elements, provide critical and historical information and insights, and ensure these knowledges are evident in students' expressive products.

Concept Formation. Art teachers also stress concept formation in art: the converting, transforming, and integration of ideas and images taken from different sources, to arrive at a new artistic concept. The altering and morphing of aesthetic schema is for most art teachers the heart of the creative process.

Open-endedness. Art teachers also use an open-ended approach to problem solving in creative forming. Students rarely are expected to replicate someone else's images or ideas, nor are their products viewed as models for others' replication. Art as an expressive activity encourages students to use multiple approaches to visual problem solving and to respond to their own visual work and the work of others in highly personal and unique ways.

Forms of inquiry. Art teachers provide students with opportunities to become engaged in forms of visual inquiry, especially through art making. They offer artistic problem-finding and problem-solving activities that may require solutions using inductive, deductive, and heuristic logic. In planning, executing, and evaluating art thought and production, students also examine many points of view; individual approaches to judging encourage students to be not only owners of their own feelings but also of their own efforts to learn.

Sequential learning. Although not all art activity requires logical or sequentially organized approaches to problem solving, nearly all forms of expressive activity do. An art maker may even deliberately create barriers to be overcome as a means of finding out the work's expressive goal. In addition to deciding strategies for accomplishing a work, the artist must consider new skills, new understandings, and new goals and order them sequentially according to the expressive end. For example, although the sequences an artist uses in making a traditional watercolor differ from those used in a scumbling search to uncover form in oil painting, both final products involve deciding on a strategy, developing new techniques, ordering a sequence of steps, and determining when that activity is ended.

Transferability of learning and variety. Teachers of art most often view the content of art production, art criticism, art history, and aesthetics as integrated in the act of conceptual forming: The knowledge gained is transferred into a single focused activity. When an art paradigm (e.g., in a schema and motif approach) is used to integrate the disciplines, all outcomes -- whether evidenced in a creative product, essay, or oral discussion -- become equal in their instructional value. This equality is due mostly to transferability, which occurs among disciplines when the goal of the activity is the creation of a new concept rather than knowledge of a concept. Art instruction is multifaceted: intake of visual perceptions, organization through the act of doing, demonstration through mastery, and creative expression through the production of original products.

Summary

Chapters 1 and 2 presented the assessment context and the need for alternative ways to assess the visual arts. Chapter 3 presented the assessment context in the school art classroom and the role of the teacher as stakeholder in the assessment process. Chapter 4 will report on teacher training and the assessment of student portfolios.

Study Questions

1. Access through using a website or find in document form the Goals 2000, and the national standards in art, and the goals and standards for your particular state. How many goals or standards do they each have and in what ways do they agree or disagree with one another?
2. What is a problem-finding behavior and how does it differ from a problem-solving behavior? Why do you think artistic activity probably involves more problem-finding activity than problem-solving activity? How would the assessment of these behaviors differ?
3. In what ways does learning in art differ from learning in the sciences? Should assessment be the same for both of these areas of study and, if not, why would their assessment differ in both their form and content?
4. What do we mean when we talk about qualitative forms of learning? What difficulties does one face in attempts to quantify qualitative learning, and given the difficulties, why would we want to do it in the first place?
5. How does Howard's (1977) typology of practice help us assess student-made objects and how does it help us to define the differences between cognitive and expressive knowledge? In your view, is knowing how to make something different from actually making something and what particular problems must be faced in assessing what it means to know and do something?
6. What makes an assessment authentic? How does an authentic assessment differ from a paper-and-pencil, true-false, or multiple-choice test? Do you think we need to use paper-and-pencil tests in assessing art performance or other forms of learning in the art classroom? Why might there be a place for both forms of evaluation in the art classroom?

References

Amabile, T. (1983). *The social theory of creativity*, New York: Springer-Verlag.

Barron, F. (1969). *Creative person and creative process*, New York: Holt, Rinehart & Winston.

Barkan, M. (1962). Transition in art education: changing conceptions of curriculum and teaching. *Art Education*, 15, 12–18.

Barron, F. (1972). *Artists in the making*. New York: Seminar Press

Bell, C. (1958). *Art*. New York: Capricorn Books.

Bruner, J. (1960). *The process of education*. Cambridge, MA: Howard University Press.

Cusic, P.A. (1994). Teachers regulating themselves and owning their own Standards. In T*he future of education perspectives on national standards* in America (P. 205–257).

N. Cobb (Ed.), New York: College Entrance Examination Board.

Dewey, J. (1934). *Art as experience*. New York: G. P. Putnam's Sons.

Eisner, E. W. (1992). The federal reform of schools: Looking for the silver bullet In *NAEA Advisory*, Reston, VA: Virginia National Art Education Association, 1–2.

Goals 2000. *Legislation.* (Public Law 103–227, 1994). Washington DC: House Document Room, Ford House Office Building.

Guilford, J. P. (1967). *The nature of human intelligence*. New York: McGraw-Hill.

Heidegger, N. (1971). *Poetry, language, thought.* New York: Harper Colophon Books.

Hope, S. (1991). Policy making in the arts and school change in *Briefing Paper*, Reston, VA; Council of Arts Accrediting Associations, 1–5

Howard, V. A. (1977). Saying it with pictures. In The arts and cognition. P. Perkins & B. Leondar (Eds.), Baltimore: The Johns Hopkins University Press. P. 208–240.

Langer, S. (1953). *Feeling and form.* New York: Charles Scribner's Sons.

National Art Education Association. (1998). NAEP and the visual arts framework, field Test and assessment. *Art Education* 51.5.

National Art Education Association. (1999). Student achievement in the arts falls short. *NAEA News* 41. (pp 1–3).

Paul, R. W. (1990). Critical and reflective thinking: A philosophical perspective. In *Dimensions of thinking and cognitive instruction*, B. F. Jones and L. Idol (Eds.). (pp. 445–493). Mahway, NJ: Lawrence Earlbaum Associates.

Perkins, D. N. (1990). *The nature and nurture of creativity.* In Dimensions of thinking and cognitive instruction (415–443). B. F. Jones and L. Idol (Eds.) Hillsdale, NJ: Lawrence Erlbaum Associates.

Slavik, S. V. (1995). *An examination of the effects of selected disciplinary art teaching strategies on the cognitive development of selected sixth grade students.* Doctoral dissertation, unpublished, Florida State University, Tallahassee.

Vermont Assessment Project. (1995). *Vermont assessment project: Focusing on the Nature of artistic practice in learning.* Montpelier, VT: Vermont Assessment Project.

4

TEACHER TRAINING AND STUDENT PORTFOLIO ASSESSMENT

Chapter 3 outlined the character of expressive learning and its assessment. This chapter will provide the reader with a basic understanding of the assessment training institutes, including the goals and activities of the project. The discussion will center on the design and methodology used by the researchers and the local considerations that made each site unique. Influences of content standards assessment practices, performance tasks, and scoring rubrics, including their links to artistic and cognitive development stages, are reported. Also to be discussed is the portfolio scoring process and the lesson plans used to implement the assessment model.

Aims of the Project

The primary consideration in the design of the student portfolio assessment part of the study was to decide whether the teacher training in three studio and curriculum development workshops would affect the art performances of the teachers' students. The portfolio assessment study sought more specifically to test the reliability of the instruments used, the procedures used to train the teachers in the assessment process, and the utility of the instruments in estimating student progress over time.

The four research questions considered were:
- Could the process systematically quantify student art performances?
- Was there interrater reliability among the teachers scoring the pre and posttest portfolios scored as a combined group?
- Were the raters' scores within each class normally distributed and did they provide sufficient score spread?
- Were the gains or losses in student portfolio scores evenly distributed among students in the lower and higher performance category?

The Study Design and Methodology

The design of the study involved the use of repeated measures on the same subjects, involving multiple observations on the same subject. The design was a one-group pretest/posttest design O X O with the students used as their own control group, compared with themselves from an earlier test. The measure before the training (B1 or pretest) represented a baseline (as control group) and the measure after the training (B2 or posttest) represented the improvement. The population consisted of students from grades pre-K to 12 and two-stage cluster sampling was used. Teachers in 51 schools in three states volunteered to participate in the study. The teacher in each school selected one class and performance assessment measures were applied on the portfolios of all students in each of the selected classes. The measures included three teacher ratings on each student art portfolio containing four works gathered before and after the teacher training.

Procedure

Each teacher collected four student artworks from the same class to form portfolio A-1 (pretest), which was scored using rubrics on a scale of 1 to 4 (4 being a high and 1 being a low) by the teacher and two additional teachers blind scoring the same portfolio. These works were again scored along with four new works gathered at the completion of the training by the teacher and the two other teachers in the study group (B-1 and B-2).

Teacher Training

Twelve two-day, pre-K–12 assessment research and development institutes were presented in Clearwater, FL, Indianapolis, IN, and Chicago, IL. The project's institutes involved 71 pre-K–12 public school art teachers for the purpose of training them to administer a field-tested, authentic pre-K–12 assessment model on student artwork, to develop and test teacher-designed assessment models for use in the cooperating school districts, to organize a data collection system for pre-K–12 student assessment, and to report the assessment data collected in formats that met individual school, school district, and state assessment standards. The institutes were conducted by art education faculty in three state universities: Florida State University in Tallahassee, FL, Purdue University in West Lafayette, IN, and Northern Illinois University in DeKalb, IL. These faculties planned the institutes and provided the assessment training portfolio development process. The research involved data from assessment instruments, questionnaires, interviews, and school observations to: (a) determine the methods and criteria used by artists, art teachers, and students with regard to how they assessed art production, (b) the effects of the assessments on teaching and learning, and (c) the impact the training had on teaching and learning and the problems encountered in its implementation.

Project Assessment Goals and Standards

Because of the research needed to reflect current national educational goals, it was necessary that the project participants become familiar with National Goals 2000 and the various art teaching standards advocated by arts professional associations, the state, and the schools charged with the responsibility of assessing the quality of instruction in American schools. It should be noted, however, that the national instructional standards in art, as published by a consortium of national arts education associations, were not necessarily the same as the standards adopted by some state departments of public instruction or those developed by the governing board of the National Assessment of Educational Progress.

Familiarity with the national standards and goals was important to both the beginning teacher and the experienced professional who knew that children and schools change over time and, to remain effective, their teaching also must reflect that change. Under the Goals 2000 mandate, art teachers are expected to match what it is they want students to learn with the national and state standards, specify which performances students are expected to achieve, and measure them accurately.

The guidelines of National Goals 2000 goals specify that:
- All children in America will start school ready to learn.
- The high school graduation rate will increase to at least 90 percent.
- All students will leave grades 4, 8, and 12 having demonstrated competency over challenging subject matter including English, mathematics, science, foreign languages, civics and government, economics, the arts, history, and geography, and every school in America will ensure that all students learn to use their minds well, so they may be prepared for responsible citizenship, further learning, and productive employment in our nation's modern economy.
- Students in the United States will be first in the world in mathematics and science achievement.
- Every adult American will be literate and will possess the knowledge and skills necessary to compete in a global economy and exercise the rights and responsibilities of citizenship.
- Every school in the United States will be free of drugs, violence, and the unauthorized presence of firearms and alcohol, and will offer a disciplined environment conducive to learning.
- The nation's teaching force will have access to programs for the continued improvement of their professional skills and the opportunity to acquire the knowledge and skills needed to instruct and prepare all American students for the next century.
- Every school will promote partnerships that will increase parental involvement and participation in promoting the social, emotional, and academic growth of children.

The Federal Content Standards.   Federal Standards were originally developed to aid educational reform in American schools.   In general, they reflect national educational concerns for knowledge transferability among disciplines, cultural diversity, and appropriate technologies, and they provide a foundation for student assessment. The content standards are, by definition, statements of what students should know and be able to do. The achievement standards specify the understandings and the levels of achievement that students are expected to attain in a given competency.   Student performances, rubrics, and anchors for evaluation that will be discussed later were based on these content and achievement standards though not explicitly evident in the standard itself. Although a standard may specify a goal, it does not explain how to reach that goal or describe what evidence is needed or from what educational products an evaluation is derived. In the language of the standard writer, the standards describe the cumulative skills and knowledge of all students upon exiting a specific grade level, but do not specify the curriculum or the activities to be used in achieving the standard that is supposedly the responsibility of the states, local school districts, and individual teachers.

Thus, although the standards are useful in at least specifying the basic performances that need to be assessed in the arts, they also must be recognized as reflecting a disciplined-based art education (DBAE) approach bias to curriculum development and assessment, which may now be what some feel is a failed program and one that has acknowledged it was designed as an in-service program for the education of curriculum generalists and was never intended to be viewed as a curriculum per se. Teachers also should be aware that the national content and achievement standards defined do not specify which artistic academic skills should be taught, how much emphasis should be given to a specific standard or how much attention, comparatively speaking, should be given among and between the standards.

The National Content Standards include (National Art Education Association, 1994):

- Understanding and applying media, technique, and process.
- Using knowledge of structures and function.
- Choosing and evaluating subject matter.
- Understanding art in relation to history and cultures.
- Reflecting on and assessing the merit of art works.
- Making connections between the visual arts and other disciplines.

State art content standards. The content standards set by individual states have greater utility for the art teacher than do the national standards. The state standards do, however, vary in number and kind. Some states have even decided not to establish any standards. Consulting the standards in any particular state is, however, the most efficient starting place for establishing school content standards and may even help simplify the process. Some states, for example, have reduced the number of standards to be achieved by compressing several different national standards into one. In Vermont, for example, the number of national art content standards has been reduced from six to four: (a) skill development, (b) reflection and critique, (c) aesthetic and critical analysis, and (d) applications to life (Vermont Arts Assessment Project, 1995). In these states, as well as in others, the standards will normally encompass the national standards, even though they may differ in their number and phraseology.

The Local School District Art Content Standards

Local school district art standards, which include both the district and individual school content standards, in some cases, will duplicate a state's art content standard and, in others, reduce or expand them in order to meet the district's policy on student assessment. Most states require the local content standards to reflect the state standards and define which art performances students are expected to engage in at different levels and how these performance are to be evaluated. The validity and reliability of these evaluations is based on their being authentic, which is to meet the criterion of fairness, requiring that students know as a part of the assigned performance task what it is they are to be evaluated on. Individual school and district-wide assessments also are expected to yield numerical data in order to provide empirical evidence that the student has achieved the content standard at a given level. Although it is questionable whether all expressive outcomes are necessarily quantifiable—that is, feelings, emotions, and beliefs—still there are a number of efficient ways to accurately estimate students' growth in the acquisition of both focal and procedural knowledge and in the power of their expressive work.

The Construction of the Assessment Instruments

To build an assessment instrument, the researchers first had to decide what it was students needed to know with a commitment to making the artistic process the primary goal and using national standards mainly as a guide. This required that the process begin with a topology of practice rather than with a set of behaviors connected to selected art world figures and their power struggles. Next, it was necessary to decide on the achievement standards specifying the student behaviors and levels of achievement to be assessed. It was recognized, however, that the national standards were more or less ideal achievements to be met at specified four-year intervals—grades 4, 8, and 12—and that they were generally based on the assumption that conceptual thinking is sequentially ordered in accordance with the hierarchy set by Bloom's taxonomy, where students move up from descriptive to analytical behaviors, that is, at grades K through 4, they know, describe, and use; at grades 5 through 8, they generalize, employ, select, analyze, and compare; and at grades 9 through 12, they conceive, evaluate, demonstrate, reflect, apply, and correlate (Bloom, 1956). Although these descriptors can be useful in setting sequential performance standards, they also assume the student will achieve those higher order thinking skills most closely associated with inductive and deductive modes of thinking. They do not, as a consequence, mention such behaviors as seeing, noticing, and performing, where at various levels students are expected to note such things as shape differences, positions, distance, and direction, to control arm movement, and to be able to paint, draw, cut, tear, measure, unfold, recombine, think metaphorically, represent, exaggerate, think symbolically, and reason metastematically.

The researchers used Howard's topology of practice in the construction of the test instruments in order to reflect the students knowing that, which is what students needed to know cognitively, and also knowing how, which is about students creating expressive objects of meaning. Neither the that nor the how was considered as more important than the other, but rather they became apparent in the unification of form and matter in the expressive object. Figure 4.1 reveals how Vernon Howard's topology of practice was used as a conceptual framework for artistic practice, where the art focal and procedural knowledge acquired could be structured so as to cohere with the national and state art content standards (Dorn, 1999). What the table effectively demonstrates is that a coherence between the national standards and what teachers actually assess in art production can occur when the assessment is constructed from a framework for practice.

Converting Art Content and Achievement Standards to Assessment Practice

Figure 4.1 shows how the National Content Standards in grades 5 through 8 were met by (a) using Howard's (1977) topology of practice to determine classroom content and achievement standards and (b) using a developmental framework of practice to determine which classroom performances can be used to evaluate the standards. Howard's to know that and to know how now become the assessment content standard, in column 2. The mental processes evolving from the achievement standards are listed in column 3. The developmentally prescribed visual performances appear in column 4 and the appropriate activities or performances also are listed in column 4. This process, in effect, reduces the six national standards to two performance standards.

Authentic Assessment

Because the instruments designed for the project primarily were needed for performance assessment, it was decided that an authentic approach would be more consistent with the assessment goals of the project. Authentic assessment requires the construction of alternative assessment items (Armstrong, 1994). Alternative assessment is considered one alternative to what is traditional (objective tests and essays). It also is focused on student performance, which is observable evidence of what students know and can do. Authentic assessment calls for authentic performances, which include real-life decisions, such as the behaviors of aestheticians, architects, art historians and critics, artists such as folk artists, people working in all forms who confront art in their daily lives, and people whose avocational activities relate to art. Authentic learning in art implies purposeful, meaningful application of relevant information, as opposed to the acquiring of factual knowledge for its own sake. It also inspires changes in curricular practices in the assessment process.

Authentic assessment is not without its critics, however. Most criticism of alternative assessments comes from the desire of test developers to have a stable population in order to acquire hard data that can be treated statistically and that can be reported as predictive or as norm-referenced scores. This requires that the student and the subject matter content to be measured also be stable and predictable. The problem is that, in any effort to assess performances in real life, the content goals are usually

Fig. 4.1. Concepts Standards for Grades 5–8

NATIONAL STANDARDS	CONCEPTUAL CONTENT STANDARDS	CONCEPTUAL ACHIEVEMENT STANDARDS	CONCEPTUAL PERFOMANCES (5–8)
Understanding and applying media		To develop a skill To routininize a process To use a skill consciously To use a process to achieve an effect	Drawing using an advanced media Make a scribbled gesture drawing Draw crushed objects Make an interlocking shape composition Create a labyrinth
Using knowledge of structures and functions	Understanding what it means to make an expressive object (procedural knowledge)	To improve in the use of a process To know the results of trials To know how a process changes a work To explain the behaviors used in the construction of a work	Make an informational drawing Use aerial perspective Juxtapose objects Remake discarded objects
Choosing and evaluating a range of subject matter		To know what historical knowledge is needed To know how to compare images To know the effects of a process To be aware of what process is used	Design a game Create a personal myth Appropriate an image Use multiple perspective
Understanding history and culture	Using knowledge of artistic process, skills, percepts, images, etc. (focal knowledge)	To know which design knowledges are required in a work To know which cultural knowledges are needed in a work	Draw something as a social commentary Interpret an ancient myth
Assessing works of art		To know historical schemas To reflect on a skill used To have a standard of achievement	Make a surrealistic image Work neoexpressionistically Create an optical illusion
Connecting with other disciplines			Create a visual pun Make science fiction art Use a science discovery as a source Create a visual paradox

unstable, mainly because in real life both the student and the content change. In art, where instructional outcomes are evident in performances designed to encourage both original and innovative responses, it is particularly hard to imagine predictable outcomes that can be generalized.

The point here is twofold. In an ill-defined field such as art, where the outcomes of instruction do not require all the students to learn the same thing in the same way, there may not be any other choice than to use alternative modes of assessment. In the construction and use of alternative assessments, art educators should also be extra careful to construct the most valid and reliable performance assessments they can make in order to insure that what it is they want students to know and do is at the center of every instructional assessment.

Developing Authentic Performance Tasks

The authentic performance tasks used in the project's assessment process were ones that grew out of the curriculum, were feasible in terms of available time and resources, and could be scored and reported in ways that satisfied teachers, parents, and administrators. The performance assessments, furthermore, were designed in such a way that they included:

- Both the procedural and focal knowledge that students needed in order for them to know how and be able to do various learning activities in the arts.
- The core performance roles or situations that all pre-K–12 students should encounter and be expected to master.
- The most salient and insightful discriminators that could be used in judging artistic performance.
- Sufficient depth and breadth to allow valid generalizations about student competence.
- The training necessary for those evaluating artistic performances to arrive at a valid and reliable assessment.
- A description of audiences that should be targeted for assessment information and how that assessment should be designed, conducted, and reported to those audiences.

Specifying Performances

In specifying the art performances to be evaluated, a number of concerns were addressed, including: how much time would be required to complete them, how many layers of investigation and content would be included, what new knowledge should be constructed, what standards were to be met, what focal and procedural knowledges were needed, and what conceptual reasoning process needed to be evident. The performances were designed to increase in complexity and range as the student matured. In other words, the layers of investigation, time, knowledge, and reasoning process would be severely limited for 4 to 7-year-old children, where the student needed only to count, notice, match, and recognize, and rather complex for 13-to 16-year-old students, where they were expected to think abstractly, reason systematically, and create new systems.

In order for the performances used to have validity, they were written and rewritten in order to identify: (a) the content standard included and (b) the conceptual (reasoning) process to be employed, that is, whether the concept was simply to recognize visual similarities or to transfigure whole forms through simplifying, changing, or disarranging them. Moreover, it took into account what focal and procedural knowledges were needed to make the standard explicit and in what kind of product it would be assessed, that is, as in a training exercise, a painting or a series of paintings, essays or critical reviews.

The most important concern in the physical design of the performance assessment was that it reflect the nature of the exercises already embedded in the art curriculum and that it encourage students to study their own train of thinking as perhaps revealed in notes, sketches, or practice efforts. Not every behavior that might be assessed is always evident in a single work that requires the performance description to specify the steps that should be followed prior to and during the execution of a work or made evident in a succession of works. Efforts to assess such things as content quality, prior knowledge, content coverage, and cognitive complexity are not always evident in every single finished work. Procedural skills, such as practice toward improvement, doing something smoothly and quickly, understanding the direction a practice session should take, controlled improvement, or getting the "feel" of something, are equally difficult to discover in a single product.

In spite of such difficulties, authentic performance assessment, therefore, is less of an intrusion on the existing curriculum because it is involved in what we normally do in instructing art. Although performance-based assessment alone may not always offer the same assessment results as conventional paper-and-pencil tests do, they are, in general, more relevant to the art instructional task and, as a consequence, are, as research results suggest, more likely to change the teacher, the student, and the curriculum for the better.

Using Rubrics in Assessment

The decision to use rubric forms for assessment came from the realization that it is the most useful in assessing what art educators generally do in the process of teaching art in schools, which is to make things and evaluate them in process. Although performance assessment is not, therefore, something really new to art teachers, the development of scoring procedures that focus on defining tasks and providing a range of points for scoring each task is new. The rubric is the scoring process most frequently used in performance assessment.

Rubrics provide a process for making a scoring decision using a cardinal or Likert-type scale that rank orders the performance being evaluated. The scale used is normally criterion referenced, which means it reaches a level of performance commensurate with what the student generally should be able to do at a particular grade level, rather than measuring some vague or absolute standard of artistic excellence. Scores derived from rubrics are more likely to indicate whether the student's achievement is above, level with, or below the standard set for what a student of a particular age and at a specific grade level should be able to achieve.

The successful use of rubrics in assessing art performances is evident in the procedures used by the Advanced Placement (AP) Examination in Studio Art exam administered by the College Entrance Examination Board and Educational Testing Service (ETS). In the AP exam, qualified art judges assess portfolios of high school student work using rubrics to produce scores as evidence that a high school student is capable of performing at grade 13 level. The AP exam is not designed as a college entrance exam, but rather as a way to recognize students in high school who already are performing at a college freshman level. Institutions of higher education that accept an AP examination score of 3 or higher offer either college credit for a beginning drawing or design course or advanced placement in the student's program.

What the AP program effectively demonstrates is that agreement can be reached among teams of art judges using rubrics to independently assess student portfolios when they are given appropriate training and effective scoring rubrics. The AP assessments have been used successfully over the past 30 years to verify that thousands of secondary art students are capable of performing at the college freshman level. As testimony of the program's success, more than 500 colleges and art schools now accept the AP studio exam score for either credit or advanced placement. One way ETS assures the comparability of the AP judges' scoring is to blindly insert freshman college-level work into the high school work being judged. More importantly, it was through the process of college art faculty reviewing the visuals in AP-scored portfolios that most colleges decided to enter the program and accept AP scores for advanced placement or credit.

Because of the nature of the tasks the project instruments needed to measure, it was decided that a holistic rubric and the AP exam model would be used to assess student art portfolios. That holistic rubrics could exist even as a mental construct was made evident in the early years of the AP studio exam, where judges were trained using a selected sample of portfolios grouped according to four scoring levels. This training process was used to provide the judges with an advanced mental gestalt of what a sample portfolio might look like at a given scoring level. The system worked well when only a few judges and a limited number of portfolios were involved. Holistic scoring in AP was introduced early in the program at the urging of artists Paul Brach and Allan Kaprow, who insisted on looking for the gestalt or "wow" factor as central in judging the students' work.

What the holistic assessment process challenged was the use of reductive measures, such as checklists, to assess individual characteristics of the work, such as the quality of line, color, balance, and unity, thus separating form from matter and divorcing what the work expressed from the means used to express it. The concern was that, whereas some students might achieve high scores on each of these points, the work as a whole might still lack in its expressive quality and aesthetic impact. Although ETS today provides its AP studio judges with a written 6-point scoring rubric with more than 38 descriptors for scoring, the method remains holistic in that the descriptions are less than exhaustive, sometimes contradictory, and not in every case needed in order to award a given score. Although most test developers agree that such holistic rubrics may be less discriminating than those that specify all the behaviors to be evaluated, it still makes a holistic approach the most truly authentic, given use of effectively trained and qualified judges.

The Design of the Scoring Rubrics

The project scoring rubric uses four sets of established criteria for scoring student portfolios or performances. It describes the four levels of performance a student might be expected to attain relative to a desired standard of achievement. It also provides performance descriptions, which tell the evaluator what characteristics or signs to look for in a student's work and how to place that work on a 4-point scale. A holistic rubric has two particular virtues. It generally communicates how the work appears in the context of other works and provides a scoring system that is easy to learn and use. The rubrics used to assess performance in grades K–12 also used maturation benchmarks that reflected higher and higher levels of performance based on both the maturity level of the student and the expectation that, as students progress, they will receive the benefits of more advanced instruction in art. Higher level (secondary) rubrics contain descriptors that reflect increasingly higher levels of thinking and visual abstraction. Holistic scoring requires a general assessment of a group of works looked at as a whole, producing a single score based on a 4-point scale.

In designing a scoring rubric:

• There should be a tight match between the demands of the performance and the criteria used in scoring.
• It should, as much as possible, specify observable aspects of the performance or product to be looked for and scored.
• It should be written in ordinary language so that assessment results can be understood.

The four scoring rubrics used in the study to measure the project's pre-K–12 art performances were designed in 1997 and field tested in three Florida school districts from 1998 to 2000. These rubrics and their construction were described in detail in Mind in Art: Cognitive Foundations in Art Education (Dorn, 1999).

Four rubrics were designed, one each for pre-K–2, 3–5, 6–8, and 9–12, and each specifying four performance levels: excellent, very good, satisfactory, and inadequate. The rubric descriptors at each level reflected age-appropriate cognitive, aesthetic, and technical skills sequentially organized. They were designed to measure performance content specified in the Florida Sunshine Standards A and B that, like the national standards, specified content in: (a) understanding and applying media techniques and processes and (b) using knowledge of structures and functions.

The performances specified in the rubrics came from three sources: Piaget's (1952) preoperational, early concrete operational. and formal operational stages; Lowenfeld's (1964) scribbling, preschematic, schematic, gang age, reasoning stage, and period of decision stage; and McFee's skill improvement stages, which include searching for pattern, using verbal descriptions of space, exploring consistencies in shape, form, and size, manipulating things as a unit, taking an average of things, completing visual wholes, and recognizing patterns in figure and ground (McFee. 1961). The performance descriptions used in constructing the rubrics were adapted from the curriculum specified in Figures. 4.2 through 4.6, first published in Dorn (1999). It should be noted that the figures include many more descriptors than used in the rubrics, which suggest that other descriptors may be used as well.

The sequential curriculum identified in Figures 4.2 through 4.6 that guided the selection of assessment criterion was designed (Dorn, 1999) to suggest what activities teachers might offer, what kinds of verbal, procedural, and cognitive abilities to develop, and which kinds of media might be appropriate for use at different levels in a school art program. The curriculum outline was arranged according to three developmental stages: (a) preconceptual, (b) conceptual/perceptual, and (b) conceptual, which are all age specific according to what might be expected given the general cognitive development stage of the learner. It should be noted, however, that concept development in one form or another will occur at all stages, even when the child only learns that the marks on the paper are by intention or when a pictorial form can be used repeatedly, as a symbol or pictogram representing a person, object, or event, both of which are evidence of conceptual growth. The distinctions in the conceptual stages used here are principally to focus on the kinds of conceptual learnings that give evidence of the students' ability to create images, to become conscious of that activity, to be able to trace it back to its origin, and to describe that process to others. These stages are used only as descriptors that fit under a preconceptual stage, indicating a consciousness of visual forms and their ordering in space, a perceptual/conceptual stage, indicating concept formation as not always being conscious and deliberate, and a conceptual stage, where visual concept formation is the main focus, even though not all children or adults may advance to this stage.

Fig. 4.2.   A suggested performance-based framework for a K–12 standards-based art curriculum including sequence, scope, and activities

STAGE 1 — PRECONCEPTUAL STAGE (ages 4–7) shape-object relationships in space			
THINKING SKILLS	FOCAL KNOWLEDGE	PROCEDURAL KNOWLEDGE	LINGUISTIC KNOWLEDGE
Knowledge Comprehension Seeing Applying	Learning: The difference between tall and wide To observe more than one object at a time To perceive shape differences To remember shape names To notice things that appear sideways, up, or down The position of things To count eyelets in shoes or openings in objects To recognize objects in area alike or different To count the number of windows in your house What things are made of To match object characteristics To differentiate words and images from objects and events about distance and direction	Learning: To control random movements To combine shapes in two- and three-dimensional forms To use simple tools To place objects on the picture plane To increase pictorial detail To paint to the edge of a shape To draw lines, shapes, and textures To make a drawing, painting, or sculpture To use different sizes and shapes of paper To use different sizes of brushes To discover thick and thin lines To repeat and vary geometric shapes To make abstract art To create big faces and little faces in crowds To cut out and place things near and far To show things in environmental space To show what it's like when it snows or rains, etc. To use crayons, chalk, and tempera paint To paste, glue, cut, and rub To make contour drawings To make maps	Learning: To apply names to shapes Words like *long, round, square, little* To talk about how things work To talk about the shapes in your house To talk about things that are closer or farther The names of tools and materials The names of colors The names of shapes To describe artworks from reproductions To identify elements in artwork To talk about lines going up and down To talk about things tall, short, round, pointed To talk about things that are near and far To talk about kinds of art, drawing, painting, etc.

Fig. 4.3. A suggested performance-based framework Conceptual/Preconceptual Early Stage of (cont.): Concrete Operation (ages 7–8)

STAGE 2 / THINKING SKILLS	CONCEPTUAL/PRECONCEPTUAL STAGE EARLY STAGE OF CONCRETE OPERATION (ages 7–8) — Recognizing similarities and locations — FOCAL KNOWLEDGE, Learning:	PROCEDURAL KNOWLEDGE, Learning:	LINGUISTIC KNOWLEDGE, Learning:
Application	To remember objects, shapes, and colors seen The differences in natural and manmade objects To break down things into smaller units About art in the community To classify things To think about things not present to vision	To invent shapes and objects To ut shapes in context through positioning To use a horizon line To draw geometric shapes To show size relationships That color varies in value To show texture	To describe objects To give names to parts of objects To explain and interpret images To know the language of judging things To know the language of preference To describe the characteristics of objects and artworks
Classifying	About objects being closer or farther away To distinguish between shapes To order shapes in an environment To understand size and shape constancies About circles and angles	To use chalks, inks, charcoal, felt tips To combine shapes and make compositions To solve space problems To use overlapping and planned color	To talk about problems To talk about speed and distance To talk about artworks, according to shapes and colors
Comparing	To see proportional size To see perspective To know the color of things To measure things To see details	To see and include detail To draw things from memory To represent activities involving friends To draw people in other places To create fantasy events	To talk about shapes, colors, lines, etc. To talk about planning The names of art tools To talk to artists about what they do
Arranging	What is tall and short To classify tools and objects To see objects from different viewpoints About sequences About expanding shapes About open and closed forms About unfolding things About grouping things About gathering things together About piling up things Forms of support such as legs and hooks	To represent figures with clothing on To represent something that happened To make landscapes To make a still life To draw the figure About gesture and mass To draw shadows About monochromatic color About pattern-negating the edge About zoom techniques, near-far To recombine shapes	

Fig 4.4. A suggested performance-based framework (cont.) : Conceptual Stage, Early Concrete Operations (ages 9–11).

STAGE 3

CONCEPTUAL STAGE
LATER STAGE OF CONCRETE OPERATIONS (ages 9–11)
Altering viewpoints/generalizing form

THINKING SKILLS	FOCAL KNOWLEDGE	PROCEDURAL KNOWLEDGE	LINGUISTIC KNOWLEDGE
	Learning:	Learning:	Learning:
Analysis	To see perspective	How to draw three dimensionally	To describe how viewpoint changes appearances
	To see and remember objects from different viewpoints	How to draw more imaginatively	To talk about distance and size of objects in art
	To consciously create symbols	To increase skill in handling tools	How to describe the relationships between things
	To see equivalent sizes in objects	To use more varied color	To describe similarities and differences in things
	To form generalizations about things observed	To use color emotionally	
Noting similarities	To see more subtle relationships between things	To draw more individualistically	How to interpret events and objects
	To apply generalizations in different settings	To represent distance through size and horizon	How to describe fantastical objects
Making abstractions	To notice size changes from different viewpoints	To paint a scene or event	To talk about paintings historically
	To think about future events	To draw shadows and receding planes	To talk about modern art
	To think about things metaphorically	To represent emotion in art	To talk about artistic styles
	To understand visual point of view	To invent metaphorical images	Terms liking *pairing* and *distributing*
	About social uses of art	To use stylistic devices	Terms such as *to cover, drape, wrap, enclose*
	To pair things	To show unusual vantage points	Terms such as *rising, falling, drooping, flowing*
	To distribute things	To use diagonals to represent planes	To describe your own art and the work of others
	What it means to scatter things	To represent things both real and imaginary	To describe similarities and differences
	To cover, drape, or wrap things	To draw things and their parts	How to make judgmental statements
	To enclose things	To use light and dark to express mood	To talk about abstract art
	To encircle things	To make gesture drawings	
	To hide things	To use tools to make prints and sculpture	
	To put curled things together in contrast	To draw groups of objects and people	
	About spreading and circling	To use various new art materials	
	About rising and falling	To represent the third dimension	
	About drooping and flowing	To make abstract art	
	About merging and dappling	To wrap and bend things	
		To make wearable art/joining shapes	
		To make like and dissimilar structures	
		To make abstractions (stylized) from nature	
		To make animated objects	
		To make crossover images in boxes	
		To make rhythmic designs	

FIG 4.5. A suggested performance-based framework (cont.) : Later Concrete Operations (ages 11–13).

STAGE 3

THINKING SKILLS	CONCEPTUAL STAGE EARLY CONCRETE OPERATIONS (AGES 11–13) FOCAL KNOWLEDGE	PROCEDURAL KNOWLEDGE	LINGUISTIC KNOWLEDGE
	Learning	Learning	Learning
Analyzing	To think analytically	To draw things with social content	To verbally describe, analyze, and evaluate works of art
	To think symbolically	To make art as a personal identification	To talk about how formal design concepts are used
	To construct mental concepts	To draw with more advanced media	To talk about art representing social issues
	To use observations more effectively	To make informational drawings	To talk about art according to artistic style
	To think creatively through problem finding	To pictorially record an event	To critique one's own work and the work of others
Decision making	To become more objective	To create architectural fantasy	
	To assess what is real and what is imagined	To create visual puns	
	To solve problems logically	To appropriate images	
	To classify, explain, and interpret events	To juxtapose objects	
Synthesis	To use criteria and concepts for judgments	To work neoexpressionistically	
	New ways to think about color	To make discarded objects	
	New approaches to subject matter	To make science-fiction art	
Problem solving	To plan and design functional objects	To make surrealistic images	
	To organize ideas historically	To create optical illusions	
	About world affairs	To create a ritual event	
	To think about things being rolled, creased, folded	To design a game	
	To think about things being twisted, intertwined	To create visual paradoxes	
	About severing things, to cut, to tear, to chip	To create labyrinths	
		To make scribbled gesture drawings	
		To use interlocking shape compositions	
		To use serial perspective	
		To use multiple perspectives	
		To make monument drawings	
		To make object sculptures	
		To draw crushed objects	
		To create personal myths	
		To interpret ancient myths	
		To use scientific discoveries as a source	

Fig 4.6. A suggested performance-based framework (cont.) : Later Concrete Operations (ages 13–16).

THINKING SKILLS	LATER CONCRETE OPERATIONS (ages 13–16) FOCAL KNOWLEDGE	PROCEDURAL KNOWLEDGE	LINGUISTIC KNOWLEDGE
	Learning:	Learning:	Learning:
Evaluation	To think abstractly To develop objective analysis To develop abstract reasoning powers To think realistically To think about the future	To create logical analogies To creae visual analogies To create texture through erasing and stippling To use arbitrary value To use contour and tone	To talk about the characteristics of an artwork To compare and contrast architectural components To describe the artistic devices and techniques
Inquiry	To think about social relationships To think inductively and deductively To reason systematically To create complex systems of mental functioning To compare relationships	To make color-field compositions To use stacked perspective To use shaped picture planes To make a drawing series	To describe the works of a given period To describe how form and content are integrated To describe the devices artists use
Experimentation	To compare representational systems and models To use metasystematic reasoning To create new systems	To make a visual narrative To make an art history series To make environmental art	To explain the effects of color in a given work To talk about art and cultural activity
Invention	To create forms of transfigurations How things look when they are agitated About art history and the various epochs To identify important artworks To compare artworks from different epochs About architectural structures To select the appropriate images	To make neonaive or bad painting To integrate nonalike forms To make a metamorphosis	

Fig. 4.7.
HOLISTIC RUBRIC FOR STANDARDS-BASED
ASSESSMENT IN THE VISUAL ARTS
Grades Pre-K–2

**EXCELLENT
LEVEL 4**

Organizes objects pictorially
Makes shapes that vary in height and width
LEVEL 4 includes multiple objects
Places shapes/objects higher and lower on the picture plane
Adds details that show the ability to count
Places objects of meaning appropriately
Provides details that show what objects are made of
Shows variety in surfaces
Represents distance and direction pictorially
Uses a variety of shapes

**VERY GOOD
LEVEL 3**

Places forms above or below each other
Uses different size shapes
Shows more than one identifiable objects
Shows some arrangement of objects on the picture plane
Provides some recognizable details
Uses geometric lines
Shows some evidence of thought in placing shapes

**SATISFACTORY
LEVEL 2**

Positions objects unrelated to their environment
Makes some variable shapes
Shows some recognizable objects
Places objects on the picture plane
Makes objects vary in their position

**INADEQUATE
LEVEL 1**

Makes shapes that generally lack structure
Makes forms that lack recognition
Provides little or no detail
Objects or shapes appear isolated

Fig. 4.8.
HOLISTIC RUBRIC FOR STANDARDS-BASED
ASSESSMENT IN THE VISUAL ARTS
Grades 3–5

EXCELLENT
LEVEL 4

Shows objects from different viewpoints
Consciously creates symbols
Generalizes things observed
Uses recombined shapes
Notes subtle relationships between objects
Makes invented shapes and objects
Shows interest in future events
Pairs and distributes similar forms
Produces fantasy pictures
Recognizes patterns
Uses geometric shapes

VERY GOOD
LEVEL 3

Makes color vary in value
Shows objects in different environments
Makes objects from memory
Reveals actual or past events
Orders similar shapes
Represents events in a literal way
Shows overlapping forms
Varies positions of objects
Sees and arranges similar shapes
Uses texture

SATISFACTORY
LEVEL 2

Places objects in relation to where work began
Makes shapes correspond with appearances
Makes shapes in isolation
Shows evidence of order

INADEQUATE
LEVEL 1

Places object randomly
Makes objects from one point of view
Uses stereotypes rather than seeking likenesses
Places shapes or objects in unrelated spaces

Fig. 4.9.
HOLISTIC RUBRIC FOR STANDARDS-BASED
ASSESSMENT IN THE VISUAL ARTS
Grades 6–8

EXCELLENT
LEVEL 4
Effectively uses elements and principles
Shows control of media
Reveals self-direction and inspiration
Uses observation, imagination, and personal feelings
Work shows both depth and scope

VERY GOOD
LEVEL 3
Frequent use of elements and principles
Generally effective, in use or media
Most often shows self-direction and inspiration
Generally employs observation, imagination, and personal feelings
Most work shows depth and scope

SATISFACTORY
LEVEL 2
Sometimes uses elements and principles
Sometimes effectively uses media
Shows some self-direction and inspiration
Sometimes communicates
Shows some involvement in the work

INADEQUATE
LEVEL 1
Little or no use of elements and principles
Little or no control of media
Little or no self-direction and inspiration
Little or no communication
Little or no involvement

Fig. 4.10.
HOLISTIC RUBRIC FOR STANDARDS-BASED
ASSESSMENT IN THE VISUAL ARTS
Grades 9–12

EXCELLENT **LEVEL 4**	Shows obvious evidence of thinking Addresses complex visual or conceptual ideas Shows inventiveness and imagination Shows experimentation and risk taking Reflects sensitivity and/or subtlety Shows excellent compositional skills Shows evidence of style and format

VERY GOOD **LEVEL 3**	Uses most elements Has some evocative qualities Shows successful engagement with some aspects of technique Demonstrates a fairly high degree of success Shows some awkwardness in some pieces Uses techniques and materials successfully Makes compositions that are strong

SATISFACTORY **LEVEL 2**	Shows an effort to solve some problems Solutions tend to be simplistic Exploration of the medium is missing Creates work that is consistently uneven Uses compositions that are weak Shows few signs of effective decision making Shows little evidence of thinking

INADEQUATE **LEVEL 1**	Uses techniques that are very poor Shows a lack of awareness of tools or media Provides solutions that tend to be trite Uses compositions that are poor or ill considered

The rubrics used in the project (Dorn, 1999), Figures 4.7 through 4.10, used a 4-point scale with a high score of 4 (excellent) and a low score of 1 (inadequate). The instruments and the adjudication process itself were modeled after the "A" quality. Program in Studio Art administered by the ETS (Askin, 1985). This approach was developed in the 1960s at the insistence of three AP planning committee artists, who argued that aesthetic judgments required holistic judgment rather than a checklist of desired behaviors. Similar approaches in the scoring of rubrics also are used by the International Baccalaureate Program and the National Board for Professional Teaching Standards.

Teacher Training in the Use of Rubrics

Project teachers were first introduced to using the rubrics through the activity of scoring sample portfolios made up of sample student artworks. They were given the opportunity to study and question the rubric descriptors and were advised that the instruments listed some, but not all, of the possible descriptors that could be used. In judging the work they also were advised that a student being scored at a given level might achieve most, but not necessarily all, of the descriptors listed for each qualitative level of performance. In the first formal adjudication, four sample portfolios were selected in advance by the researchers and were scored by three project teachers, with the other project teachers in the group looking on. Afterward, the teachers discussed where they agreed and disagreed. The samples were discussed at the pre-K–2, 3–5, 6–9, and 10–12 levels. This benchmarking process preceded each adjudication conducted in the project.

Fig. 4.11. Student portfolio samples—excellent, very good, satisfactory, inadequate.

student portfolios—excellent

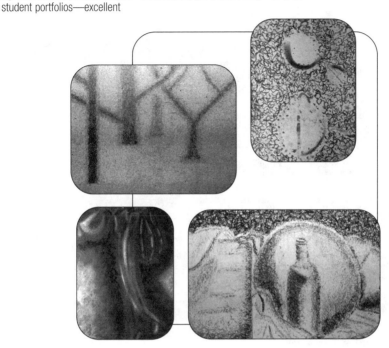

student portfolios—very good

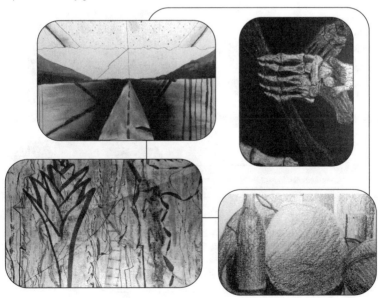

Fig. 4.11. Student portfolio samples—excellent, very good, satisfactory, inadequate (cont.)

student portfolios—satisfactory

student portfolios—inadequate

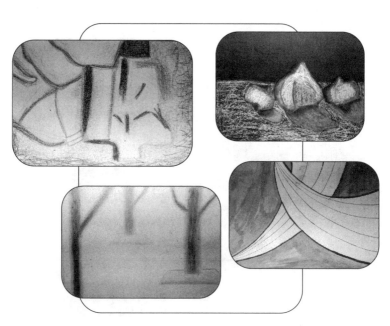

Deciding What Would Be Judged

Project teachers were expected to judge student portfolios containing four different two-dimensional works, that is, drawings or paintings selected by the teacher or the student to represent a "body" of work. The portfolios included four works using a variety of media and subject matter. The decision to use varied works rather than works reflecting common assignments was intended to reflect what actually occurs in American schools, where art teachers make different assignments and art students solve visual problems in different ways.

The Gestalt Method

When scoring the portfolios, the teachers were instructed that the rubric, which was reviewed at the start, was only to be used as a guide and reviewed only as needed in the adjudication process. The teachers were told to apply the rubrics holistically, judging four works as a whole and giving a single score guided by the benchmark training session and their own intuitive understanding of expressive forming as artists and as teachers familiar with the art performances of K–12 students at a given level. The teachers were cautioned that this judgment process was to be used in order to assess the expressive quality of the four works as a whole, rather than to apply a reductionist scoring method that evaluated elements, principles, and techniques. They also were advised that the method of using a checklist to obtain objective scoring, although producing valid scores all too frequently overlooked the qualitative Gestalt or "hair on the back of the neck" sense of the power of the expressive object.

Score Spread

The teachers also were advised that they should plan to use all four scoring levels in their assessment, including at least a few 1s (low) and 4s (high). The benchmark sampling activity preceding the scoring process was used as a guideline to help the teachers mentally envision how student works could be evaluated on a 4-point scale, where a portfolio of works of outstanding quality would receive a score of 4 and a portfolio of works of low quality would receive a 1. A score of 3 would then be given to works that would be on the high side, but not as strong as a 4 and a score of 2 would be given to works on the low side, but not as weak as a 1. See Figure 4.11.

The benchmark-sample trainings were repeated until all the teachers in the group generally agreed on which portfolios constituted a 4, a 3, a 2 and a 1.

Portfolio Assessment Plan

The project required each teacher to select one of their classes to be included in the study over a 4 to 8 month period. They were told to organize two portfolios of four works for each student, one collected at the beginning of the year and a second collected at the end of the course, either in January or April. The first student portfolio adjudication (A-1) was adjudicated in the fall by the students' teacher and by two other project teachers. The choice to ask the teacher to score the portfolio in the A-1 rating was both to ascertain the teacher's ability to independently score the portfolio and to provide a dialogue between the teacher and the other independent raters as to the need for objectivity in the rating process. The A-1 scoring results indicated that, although teachers who scored their own students' work had a high level of agreement with the independent judges, more often than not they scored their own students' work either somewhat higher or lower. During the process, some teachers had difficulty in objectively scoring their own students' work according to its overall expressive quality, preferring in some cases to score the work on how well the student followed the teacher's instructions or how much improvement the student had made over previous assignments. The ensuing dialogue between the teachers and the other raters helped make it clear that works that do not follow a teacher's lesson plan still may be powerfully expressive. Most teachers did, however, have difficulty reconciling the work of children with disabilities with the other children in the class. It was decided, however, that, in this project, the portfolios of these children would be viewed on the same basis as the other children in the class.

Insuring Score Spread

The project teachers were advised in scoring the portfolios that they also needed to think about achieving sufficient score spread in judging the portfolios to insure that the judges were discriminating by giving scores at the 1, 2, 3, and 4 levels. They also were told to expect that, in the portfolios they assessed, there would be at least a few 1 and 4 scores, although the majority of scores given would probably be at the 2 and 3 levels. The choice to use a 4- rather than a 5-point rubric was made to avoid a situation in which teachers did not make critical decisions and scored most of the work in the middle of the scoring rubric. Earlier pilot studies of art teachers using these instruments indicated that art teachers more often than not scored the portfolios in the upper two quartiles of the scoring range, thus producing a skewed distribution rather than a normal-probability bell-shaped curve distribution.

Interjudge Reliability

In scoring the portfolios, teachers were further advised during the benchmark-sample training sessions that a 1-point difference in scores between two different judges was acceptable, but that a score difference of 2 or more points would suggest that the judges may not be looking at the same features in the works. These disagreements would indicate what AP portfolio testers call "reader fatigue," where judges become unfocused because they are tired or need a break. When this happened with some frequency, the adjudication was be stopped in order to give the group a break or to give individuals or the whole group additional benchmark training. The 1-point difference standard has been used by ETS in the studio art program and similar measures are employed in the International Baccalaureate. Where assessment raters continue to show a high level of discrepancy with other raters, different portfolio assessment programs solve the problem in different ways. One program seeks agreements among the raters in order to change their scores. A second program calls for a chief scorer to change the scores arbitrarily. A third program requires the judges to undergo pretraining activities and, when they too frequently disagree with other raters, they are dismissed in advance or, if used, not invited to return. This project followed the AP approach, which is to ask the raters whether they would like to change their scores or leave them as they were originally scored.

Discrepancies

When judges disagreed by more than 1 point, the adjudication leader asked the two judges to take a second look at the portfolio to see if they could remember what score they had given it. In most cases, one judge or the other decided to give it a different score from the one originally given. One or both of the judges most often decided to change their scores to agree within a point, but some judges would, however, stick with their original rating and in such cases the scores were left as they were originally scored. Discrepancies occurred in about 5% of each round of group adjudication. Considering that in some of these adjudications teachers as a group reviewed up to 500 portfolios containing 2,000 artworks and that they did this three times for each portfolio, requiring 6,000 independent observations, some fatigue and disagreement among the raters was normally expected.

Field Tests of the Project Instruments

A field test of the instruments and the assessment training used in the project was conducted in 1999 in Dade and Brevard County, FL, schools. Two hypotheses were generated for statistical analysis of the data from the field tests in order to determine: (a) if the instruments discriminated between the performances of students on a scale of 1 to 4 and (b) whether the art teachers' scoring of their own students' work differed significantly from the independent ratings of at least two other judges' blind scoring the same work.

Method

Subjects. Subjects included 216 students, from the Dade and Brevard school districts, who created 864 student works. Eighteen art teachers, nine in each district, participated in scoring the works.

Results of the Field Test

Fig. 4.12. Pinellas County art teachers scoring student art portfolios.

Reliability. The scores of the art teacher (Judge 1) and the two independent judges (Judge 2 and Judge 3) for the Brevard and Dade school districts were subjected to a Kruskal-Wallis H test to determine if any significant differences existed between the judges' scores within each grade level (pre-K–2, 3–5, 6–9, and 9–12). No significant differences were found at any grade level for either school district. A probability at a .05 confidence level, as typically used in statistical analysis, was set as the cutoff point for determination of significant differences.

Score spread. A score of 3, on a 4-point scale, was given in 30 to 40% of the cases at all grade levels in both school districts, whereas a score of 1, on a 4-point scale, was given between 8 and 15% of the time. Most of the agreement in the judges' scores, when compared across all grade levels in both districts, occurred between the scores of 2 and 3.

Interjudge reliability. A Spearman's rho correlation was performed on the scores of the art teacher and each of the independent judges, at each grade level, in order to determine the relationships between the judges' scores. The results indicated a significant level of agreement (p. 01) between the art teacher and Judge 2 or Judge 3 at all grade levels in both school districts.

Overall, the combined results from the Kruskal-Wallis H test and Spearman rho correlation indicate consistent scoring by the judges and a high level of agreement, respectively, in judging the artwork within each grade level and school district. Finally, the range of scoring demonstrated sufficient variability and use of the full 4-point rating scale by the judges.

Conclusions of the Field Tests

Although additional field testing of the rubric instruments was recommended, a statistical analysis of the scores accorded by the judges suggested a significant level of agreement among all the judges on the scores given the 216 portfolios and sufficient range, variability, and use of the full 4-point scale. These results suggest that the rubrics, when administered by teachers trained in a gestalt scoring process, can produce reliable estimates of student artistic performance. They also suggest that individual teachers scoring their own students' work would produce reliable test scores, as evidenced by the number of the times the same assessment was given the same scores when repeated by other judges (Beattie, 1997).

Fig. 4.13. Pinellas County art teachers scoring student art portfolios.

Validity. A number of factors suggested that the rubrics produced a valid estimate of student art performance. The principal factor was that the items being judged were the direct products of the instructional program and, as artworks, were consistent with the ends and means of art and were a product of artistic inquiry. In addition, the purpose of the assessment was relevant to the performance being evaluated, is relevant to the discipline being assessed, and was created in a climate that provided equal opportunities for all students to succeed and was motivated by the students' own expressive desires.

Straightforwardness. The rubrics also were designed using a taxonomy of increasing cognitive complexity in student achievement in grades K–12. Because the assessed artwork was an outgrowth of what the student was expected to know and be able to do, the assessment was straightforward about what was expected and was cohesive in that what the student was expected to know was evident in the products of artistic inquiry that were assessed.

Efficiency. As a practical matter, the assessment process that would ideally be conducted by art teachers should be efficient and cost effective. The process would involve art teachers in doing what they normally do in teaching art, which is to provide motivation and instruction, observe the products of instruction, critique the class and individual students, and change the instructional environment if necessary. Instructional time would not be interrupted by taking and administering tests. No standardized or printed tests would need to be purchased or scored and the reporting of results would be made evident principally in the improved quality of student artwork.

Reliability.   Reliability is defined as the consistency of test scores, which can be demonstrated in how many times the same assessment, when repeated under the same conditions, would be given the same scores. In this experiment, the same portfolio of work was judged and scored by the teacher and at least two other art teachers. In most cases, there was an 85% to 90% agreement on the scores given by three judges scoring the work independently. Because these three rater scores correlated well, it was determined that there was a high degree of interrater reliability.

Cohesiveness. Finally, the issue of cohesiveness, which refers to the homogeneity of exercises between what some support as four distinct underlying disciplines, is unresolved and open to debate. Much of the debate centers on the issue of whether art education is concerned with the expressive aesthetic development of students or with the preparation of students in the separate disciplines of studio production, art history, criticism, and aesthetics. The debate will not be resolved through testing. More importantly, the preliminary findings of the study suggest that teachers using these rubrics and using the judgement training employed in this case would in the future produce reliable judgements of pre-K–12 art student performance.

Project Portfolio Goals

The portfolio assessment part of the project had essentially two major goals. The first was to develop a process whereby teachers could learn to accurately assess student art performances in the context of what different school art programs with different curricula and different students actually do. The second goal was to develop a teacher inservice education program that would focus on enhancing teachers' own creative work and on using this enhancement to improve the quality of their teaching and subsequently the quality of their own students' work. This was accomplished in two ways: (a) hands-on workshops in creative forming and (b) developing new studio curricula for the art classroom. Three half-day studio workshops were offered at three project sites in Florida and Indiana. The Illinois project focused on portfolio development.

The teacher studio workshops, taught by secondary art teachers, studio artists, and college-level art instructors, offered three intensive studio workshop sessions on drawing from the figure, drawing and painting from still-life subject matter, and creating an imaginative abstract work. The three sites differed slightly in what was presented and on what goals were to be accomplished, but all focused on engaging in basic studio practices in observational drawing, the use of appropriate media, and imaginative ways of approaching art content and form. Each project site teacher was presented with model lessons on the three topics developed by Nancy Dillon, an art teacher at Brevard (FL) Community College who field tested the lessons with a group of teachers in Brevard County, Florida, in 2000.

Although each site approached the studio problems in different ways, all provided some skill training, an introduction to the use of art media, drawing from observation and from imagination, problem assignments, and follow-up critiques of the teachers' work. The teachers also received lesson plan handouts, a vocabulary of terms, slides showing examples of both students' and professional artists' approaches to the problem, suggested resources, and, in some cases, duplicate slides of student works that could be used in lesson plan development.

Figures 4.14, 4.15, and 4.16 are examples of the handouts provided by Pat Priscoe of Pinellas County Schools and a workshop instructor. Figure 4.14 is an outline of her workshop plan in abstract drawing, Fig. 4.15, an example of a written examination on abstract art for the student, and Fig. 4.16, a student self-evaluation of an abstract drawing project.

Fig. 4.14. Abstract Drawing and Mixed Media Workshop

ABSTRACT DRAWING AND MIXED MEDIA WORKSHOP		
AIM	GOAL	RESULTS
Florida Sunshine State Standards Skill and technique Creation & communication Cultural & historical connections Aesthetic & critical analysis Application to life	1. Demonstrate a historical understanding of abstract art. 2. Demonstrate an understanding of similarities and differences within the style of abstract art. 3. Demonstrate coexistence of perceptual and conceptual imagery to produce a work of art. 4. Effective use of space in an abstract composition. 5. Demonstrate use of mixed medias to produce an abstract work of art.	progress process evaluation/critique rubric critical analysis summative evaluation posttest

HUMAN RESOURCES	PROCESSES	INFORMATION & ANALYSIS
Art reproductions & acetate transparencies Art books Handouts	1. View and discuss examples of abstract compositions. 2. Identify qualities/attributes of the abstract art style. 3. Compare similarities and differences within abstract art style. 4. Establish criteria to be achieved (goals). 5. Create a contour drawing of something observed on foam core using black crayon or marker (i.e., object, plant hand, feet, or face). 6. Glue down torn tissue paper. 7. Dry. 8. Embellish surface with white and/or black ink or paint. 9. Critical analysis/summative assessment. 10. Grade level variations on project.	Pretest/Posttest

Fig. 4.15. Attributes of Abstract Art

Name _____
Date _____
Class _____

ATTRIBUTES OF ABSTRACT ART

Directions:
1. Write a working definition for each style of art listed below.
2. Read pp. 158–161, *The Annotated Mona Lisa*, and list at least FIVE attributes in the space below.

Definitions:
Abstract — Artwork, based on recognizable objects, presented in a highly stylized manner that stresses the elements of art and principles of design.
Abstract Expressionism — A 20th century art style of the late 1940's and early 1950's that rejected the use of recognizable subject matter and emphasized the spontaneous process of expression and creating art.
Nonobjective/Non-representational Art — Art that has no recognizable objects or subject matter. The actual subject matter might be color or the composition of the work itself.

Elements of Art	Principles of Design
Line	Balance
Shape/Form	Repetition/Pattern
Value	Unity
Color	Contrast
Texture	Emphasis
Space	Rhythm/Movement
	Proportion

Fig. 4.16. Mixed Media Abstract Art Rubric

MIXED MEDIA ABSTRACT ART RUBRIC Name _____

Class _____

Date _____

Direction to student: Read rating scale to be used to grade the listed criteria for a successful mixed media abstract art assignment.

Rating Scale:

4 = Excellent, Outstanding Achievement
3 = Very Good, Above Average Achievement
2 = Average, Acceptable Achievement
1 = Barely Average, Needs Improvement, Limited Achievement
0 = Unfinished, Not attempted

1. Accurately drew a contour drawing of an object, plant, face or hand on to foam core board with black marker.
   4   3   2   1   0

2. Used a black crayon to make various texture rubbings on tissue paper.
   4   3   2   1   0

3. Effectively adhered torn pieces of tissue paper over contour drawing on foam core board.
   4   3   2   1   0

4. Effectively used paint to embellish surface of tissue paper to enhance contrast.
   4   3   2   1   0

5. Effectively used paint to embellish surface of tissue paper to enhance visual balance creating a mixed media abstract art composition.
   4   3   2   1   0

6. Name is on the picture plane of the art work.
   4   3   2   1   0

Total and divide by 6 = _____ average

CRITICAL ANALYSIS: Answer in complete sentences.

1. A. What did you discover about abstract art that you did not know before?

    B. How did you discover it?

2. A. What was your biggest challenge in creating your mixed media abstract work of art?

    B. How did you work through it?

3. A. What successes did you experienced in creating an abstract work of art?

    B. How did you achieve them?

4. Identify the different abstract art attributes and they were used in the creating of your mixed media abstract work of art?

Workshop Organization

The project directors, with the assistance of school district leaders, offered 18 project workshops ranging from .5 to 2 days in length. The workshops were conducted in St. Petersburg and Miami, Florida, Mundelein, Illinois, and Indianapolis, Indiana during the fall and spring of 2000 to 2001. The activities included special lectures, assessment training, studio activities, critiques of teacher and student work, curriculum planning, and group discussions. The Florida and Indiana sites focused on studio workshops and curriculum planning, whereas the Illinois workshop focused on alternative portfolio development. Although the agendas differed at the various sites, they all included assessment training and the scoring of student art portfolios.

Fig. 4.17. Dade County art teacher drawing from the model.

The 1- or 2-day workshops in Florida and Illinois were supported by either inservice funds and credits from the school districts or project funds, with the half-day sessions occurring mostly in Indiana as after-school or evening workshops where teachers volunteered to meet in different locations in the city. The workshops in Florida occurred in two separate school districts, whereas the Indiana workshop included teachers from two different school districts and, in Illinois, from 11 different school districts. Attendance in the workshops ranged from 12 to 20 teachers for each workshop.

Fig. 4.18.

PRECONCEPTUAL STAGE (ages 4–7) Shape-object relationships in space	**GOALS** Highlight two or more of the focal and procedural knowledges on the left you wish to emphasize in this lesson. What other goals do you wish to accomplish?

PRECONCEPTUAL STAGE (ages 4–7)
Shape-object relationships in space

FOCAL KNOWLEDGE
Learning:

The difference between tall and wide

To observe more than one object at a time

To perceive shape differences

To remember shape names

To notice things that appear sideways, up, or down

The position of things

To count eyelets in shoes or openings in objects

To recognize objects that are alike or different

To count the number of windows in your house

What things are made of

To match object characteristics

To differentiate words & images from objects & events

About distance and direction

PROCEDURAL KNOWLEDGE
Learning:

To control random movements

To combine shapes in two-and three-dimensional forms

To use simple tools

To place objects on the picture plane

To increase pictorial detail

To paint to the edge of a shape

To draw lines, shapes, and textures

To make a drawing, painting, or sculpture

To use different sizes and shapes of paper

To use different sizes of brushes

To discover thick and thin lines

To repeat and vary geometric shapes

To make abstract art

To create big faces and little faces in crowds

To cut out and place things near and far

To show things in environmental space

To show what it's like when it snows or rains, etc.

To use crayons, chalk, and tempera paint

To paste, glue, cut, and rub

To make contour drawings

To make maps

GOALS
Highlight two or more of the focal and procedural knowledges on the left you wish to emphasize in this lesson. What other goals do you wish to accomplish?

MOTIVATION
What artists or student works will you use as examples to motivate student interest in achieving the goals of this assignment?

What drawing techniques and organizational skills will you demonstrate to the class?

What materials and tools will you need to conduct the assignment?

What steps (if any) do you expect your students to take and to think about in the process of completing this assignment?

Fig. 4.19.

CONCRETE OPERATIONAL STAGE (ages 7–8)
Recognizing similarities and locations

FOCAL KNOWLEDGE

Learning:
To remember objects, shapes, and colors seen
The differences in natural and man-made objects
To break down things into smaller units
About art in the community
To classify things
To think about things not present to vision
About objects being closer or farther away
To distinguish between shapes
To order shapes in an environment
To understand size and shape constancies
About circles and angles
To see proportional size
To see perspective
To know the color of things
To understand families and classes of things
To measure things
To see details
What is tall and short
To classify tools and objects
To see objects from different viewpoints
About sequences
About expanding shapes
About open and closed forms

PROCEDURAL KNOWLEDGE

Learning:
To invent shapes and objects
To put shapes in context through positioning
To use a horizon line
To draw geometric shapes
To show size relationships
That color varies in value
To show texture
To use chalks, inks, charcoal, felt tips
To combine shapes and make compositions
To solve space problems
To use overlapping and planned color stages
To see and include detail
To draw things from memory
To represent activities involving friends
To draw people in other places
To create fantasy events
To represent figures with clothing on
To represent something that happened
To make landscapes
To make a still life
To draw the figure
About gesture and mass

GOALS
Highlight two or more of the focal and procedural knowledges on the left you wish to emphasize in this lesson. What other goals do you wish to accomplish?

_____
_____
_____

MOTIVATION
What artists or student works will you use as examples to motivate student interest in achieving the goals of this assignment?

_____
_____
_____

What drawing techniques and organizational skills will you demonstrate to the class?

_____
_____
_____

What materials and tools will you need to conduct the assignment?

_____
_____

What steps (if any) do you expect your students to take and to think about in the process of completing the assignment?

_____
_____
_____
_____
_____
_____
_____
_____
_____
_____
_____

Fig. 4.20.

CONCRETE OPERATIONS (ages 9–11)

FOCAL KNOWLEDGE

Learning:
To see perspective
To see and remember objects from different viewpoints
To consciously create symbols
To see equivalent sizes in objects
To form generalizations about things observed
To see more subtle relationships between things
To apply generalizations in different settings
To notice size changes from different viewpoints
To think about future events
To think about things metaphorically
To understand visual point of view
About social uses of art
To pair things
To distribute things
To see complimentary things
What it means to scatter things
To cover, drape, or wrap things
To enclose things
To encircle things
To hide things
To put curled things together in contrast
About spreading and circling
About rising and falling
About drooping and flowing

PROCEDURAL KNOWLEDGE

Learning:
To draw three dimensionally
How to draw more imaginatively
To increase skills in handling tools
To use more varied color
To use color emotionally
To draw more individualistically
To represent distance through size and horizon
To paint a scene or event
To draw shadows and receding planes
To represent emotion in art
To invent metaphorical images
To use stylistic devices
To show unusual vantage points
To use diagonals to represent planes
To represent things both real and imaginary
To draw things and their parts
To use light and dark to express mood
To make gesture drawings
To use tools to make prints and sculpture
To draw groups of objects and people
To use various new art materials
To represent the third dimension
To make abstract art
To wrap and bend things

GOALS
Highlight two or more of the focal and procedural knowledges on the left you wish to emphasize in this lesson. What other goals do you wish to accomplish?

_____

_____

_____

MOTIVATION
What artists or student works will you use as examples to motivate student interest in achieving the goals of this assignment?

_____

_____

_____

What drawing techniques and organizational skills will you demonstrate to the class?

_____

_____

_____

What materials and tools will you need to conduct the assignment?

_____

_____

_____

What steps (if any) do you expect your students to take and to think about in the process of completing the assignment?

_____

_____

_____

_____

_____

_____

_____

_____

_____

_____

_____

FIG. 4.21.

CONCRETE OPERATIONS (ages 11–13)	
FOCAL KNOWLEDGE	

Learning:
To think analytically
To think symbolically
To construct mental concepts
To use observations more effectively
To think creatively through problem finding
To become more objective
To assess what is real and what is imagined
To solve problems logically
To classify, explain, and interpret events
To use criteria and concepts for judgments
New ways to think about color
New approaches to subject matter
To plan and design functional objects
To organize ideas historically
About world affairs

PROCEDURAL KNOWLEDGE	

Learning:
To draw things with social content
To make art as a personal identification
To draw with more advanced media
To make informational drawings
To pictorially record an event
To create architectural fantasy
To create visual puns
To appropriate images
To juxtapose objects
To work neoexpressionistically
To remake discarded objects
To make science-fiction art
To make surrealistic images
To create optical illusions
To create a ritual event
To design a game
To create visual paradoxes
To create labyrinths
To make scribbled gesture drawings
To use interlocking shape compositions
To use aerial perspective
To use multiple perspectives
To make monument drawings
To make object sculptures
To draw crushed objects
To create personal myths
To interpret ancient myths
To use scientific discoveries as a source

GOALS
Highlight two or more of the focal and procedural knowledges on the left you wish to emphasize in this lesson. What other goals do you wish to accomplish?

——————————
——————————
——————————

MOTIVATION
What artists or student works will you use as examples to motivate student interest in achieving the goals of this assignment?

——————————
——————————

What drawing techniques and organizational skills will you demonstrate to the class?

——————————
——————————

What materials and tools will you need to conduct the assignment?

——————————
——————————
——————————

What steps (if any) do you expect your students to take and to think about in the process of completing the assignment?

——————————
——————————
——————————
——————————
——————————
——————————
——————————
——————————
——————————
——————————

Fig. 4.22.

CONCRETE OPERATIONS (ages 13–16)

FOCAL KNOWLEDGE

Learning:

To think abstractly
To develop objective analysis
To develop abstract reasoning powers
To think realistically
To think about the future
To think about social relationships
To think inductively and deductively
To reason systematically
To create complex systems of mental functioning
To compare relationships
To compare representational systems and models
To use metasystematic reasoning
To create new systems
To create forms of transfigurations
How things look when they are agitated
About art history and the various epochs
To identify important artworks
To compare artworks from different epochs
About architectural structures
To select the appropriate images

PROCEDURAL KNOWLEDGE

Learning:

To create logical analogies
To create visual analogies
To create texture through erasing and stippling
To use arbitrary value
To use contour and tone
To make color-field compositions
To use stacked perspective
To use shaped picture planes
To make a drawing series
To make a visual narrative
To make an art history series
To make environmental art
To make neonaive or bad painting
To integrate nonalike forms
To make a metamorphosis

GOALS
Highlight two or more of the focal and procedural knowledges on the left you wish to emphasize in this lesson. What other goals do you wish to accomplish?

MOTIVATION
What artists or student works will you use as examples to motivate student interest in achieving the goals of this assignment?

What drawing techniques and organizational skills will you demonstrate to the class?

What materials and tools will you need to conduct the assignment?

What steps (if any) do you expect your students to take and to think about in the process of completing the assignment?

The workshop formats in Florida and Indiana generally included 3 to 4 hours of studio activity, 1 to 2 hours of curriculum development, and 1 hour of reviewing sample student work inspired by the lesson plans developed from the previous workshop. The general plan was to offer the teachers an intensive studio workshop, followed by a critique of the teachers' work, to develop lesson plans based on the workshop adapted to each teacher's grade level, and to review and share student artwork completed in the period between the workshops, which were spaced from 4 to 6 weeks apart.

Fig. 4.23. Dade County art teachers preparing a tissue paper collage background for an abstract drawing.

Curriculum Development

At the conclusion of the studio workshop, teachers in the Indiana and Florida school sites began the process of constructing lesson plans based on what they had learned in the studio session as it might apply to their classes. In order to assist the teachers in lesson planning, they were presented with the curriculum guidelines 4.18 through 4.22 which summarized the focal and procedural knowledges contained in the curriculum on which the rubrics were based for age groups 4–7, 7–8, 9–11, 11–13, and 13–16, with suggestions about goals, motivation, materials, equipment, and procedures. Teachers could choose to follow that outline or adapt it to their district's or their own individual lesson plans.

The lesson plans developed by Pinellas County teachers were developed in several different formats including, an elementary drawing lesson developed by Nancy Keyton, Figure 4.24, a secondary level still-life drawing and a mixed-media abstract project by Pat Prisco, Figures 4.25–26, a still life drawing lesson plan by Donna Sinicrope Figure 4.27 for a second-grade drawing project.

Fig. 4.24.

NANCY KEYTON ◆◆◆ ART EDUCATION

ACTIVITY/LESSON   DRAWING WHITE CLOUD

LEVEL 4
LESSON LENGTH
1–2 SESSIONS

SKILL/TECHNIQUES VA.A

CULTURAL/HISTORICAL VA.C

APPLICATION TO LIFE VA.E

CREATION/COMMUNICATION VA.B

AESTHETIC/CRITICAL ANALYSIS VA.D

ELEMENTS
line   **shape/form**
color   **value**
texture   **space**

LESSON OBJECTIVES VA.A

LEARNING TO DRAW THE HUMAN FACE

TO OBSERVE THE PROPORTIONS OF THE
FACE

TO LEARN ABOUT THE NATIVE AMERICANS
IN THE EARLY WEST AND THE ARTIST
GEORGE CATLIN

⇈⇈⇈⇈⇈

RESOURCES/MATERIALS VA.C/VA.E
  F.S. AMERICAN WESTWARD MOVEMENT
  READING AND O'REILLY

  PRINT-WHITE CLOUD, CHIEF OF THE
  IOWAS

  PENCILS AND COLORED PENCILS

PRINCIPLES
Emphasis
Contrast
Unity
Balance
Rhythm & movement
Proportion
Repetition & pattern

VOCABULARY
PROPORTIONS
SKETCH
OBSERVE
IOWA
JEFFERSON MEDAL
WESTWARD MOVEMENT

ACTIVITY PROCESSES/PROCEDURES VA.B

AFTER VIEWING FILMSTRIPS STUDENTS
WILL CRITIQUE GEORGE CATLIN'S PAINTING

OBSERVING HIS DRESS AND THE
PROPORTIONS OF HIS FACE TO THEIR OWN
FACE

STUDENT WILL UNDERSTAND SOME ARTIST
RECORD HISTORY.

ASSESSMENT METHOD VA.D

TEACHER OBSERVATION

DID THEY TRY TO RECORD AS MUCH AS
THEY COULD OF WHITE CLOUD'S FACE
AND DRESS USING THE PROPORTIONS
WE DISCUSSED?

Fig. 4.25.

Activity / Lesson: STILL LIFE DRAWING	Lesson Length: 8–10 classes

Strands — Standards — Benchmarks: (check and fill)   **Media** (check)

X   Skills/Techniques — VA.A 1.4._1_, 1.4._2_, 1.4._3_, 1.4._4_   __ Collage

X   Creation/Communication — VA.B 1.4._2_, 1.4._4_, 1.4.__, 1.4.__   __ Computer Graphics

X   Cultural/Historical Connections — VA>C 1.4._1_, 1.4.__   x_ Drawing

X   Aesthetic/Critical Analysis — VA.D 1.4._2_. 1.4.__, 1.4.__   __ Fibers

X   Application to Life — VA.E 1.4._2_, 1.4.__, 1.4.__   __ Jewelry

     __ Mixed Media

     __ Painting

     __ Photography

     __ Printmaking

     __ Sculpture (3-D)

Lesson Objectives — What the student is going to learn:
The student will enhance their perceptual skills and graphite pencil techniques to effectively use value variations to create a 2-D drawing of a 3-D observed still life consisting of black, gray, and white arranged objects.

Activity Processes and Procedures:
1. Teacher introduces still life drawing to students by lecturing on the history of still lifes and a discussion analyzing the compositional and technique qualities of two different styles of still lifes.
2. Teacher presents samples of still life pencil drawings and leads a discussion on comparing and contrasting strong and weak compositional choices and pencil techniques. Draw from students' recent experiences of using pencil weights, pencil pressure, and pencil techniques in previous pencil technique shading assignment. Through discussion achievement expectations are established by students through a teacher directed analysis. Write on board.
3. Direct students to frame out 12"x12" white drawing paper creating a 1" margin.
4. Direct students to diagram and shade in using a pencil smooth shading technique a 6 section gradation scale using varied pencil pressures with two different pencil weights (4H and HB). Have students reference their pencil technique paper.
5. Teacher gives a demonstration of using viewfinder to isolate and select part of still life to be drawn. Review good compositional qualities with emphasis on balance. Teacher demonstrates a lightly drawn contour drawing of a selected compositional choice from a still life arrangement of white, gray, and black objects forms. Lecture on how to look for underlying geometric shapes to better achieve accuracy of drawing observed forms. (Note: it is easier for beginning students to transfer observed values to pencil pressures observing a still life arrangement of white, gray, and black objects).
6. Students use viewfinders to lightly draw the contours of observed objects of chosen part of still life arrangement. Teacher checks contour drawing before student begins shading.
7. Teacher demonstrates shading initial values on paper emphasizing layering from light to dark values as they did on their pencil technique papers.
8. Students shading in still life drawing beginning with 4H pencil and moving on to HB when darker values are needed. Teacher reminds students that no outlines, only value creating edges of forms.
9. At a midpoint, all drawings are placed on board and a teacher directed discussion is conducted to analyze beginning use of layering values to produce gradual change in values and not dramatic bands. Give pointers on how to correct.
10. Students continue shading in drawing. Teacher directs students to create shadows as if they were a shape connected to object and to check highlight areas.
11. Teacher directs students to clean up of finger smudges and highlights and crisp up edges without adding a line to finished drawing.
12. Evaluate and critique.

Fig. 4.26.

Activity/Lesson: Mixed Media Abstract Art	Lesson Length: 4 – 5 classes

Strands — Standards — Benchmarks:
X Skills/Techniques – VA.A 1.4.1, 1.4.2, 1.4.3, 1.4.4
X Creation/Communication – VA.B 1.4.1, 1.4.2, 1.4.3. 1.4.4
X Cultural/Historical Connections – VA.C 1.4.1, 1.4.2
X Aesthetic/Critical Analysis – VA.D 1.4.1, 1.4.2, 1.4.__
X Application to Life – VA.E 1.4.2, 1.4.__, 1.4.__

Media (check)
x_ Collage
__ Computer Graphics
x_ Drawing
__ Fibers
__ Jewelry
x_ Mixed Media
x_ Painting
__ Photography
__ Printmaking
__ Sculpture (3-D)

Lesson Objectives — What the student is going to learn:
The student will combine their perceptual skills and conceptual skills effectively by using a mixed media process to create an abstract work of art.

Activity Processes and Procedures:
1. Teacher introduces Abstract Art to students by viewing, discussing, and analyzing the compositional and technique qualities of student examples of abstract mixed media works of art. Write on board.
2. Each student is given art history research and attribute worksheet as a class assignment. Students use art history books to complete assignment. Students turn in for teacher evaluation.
3. In small groups of four, students fill in *Similarities and Differences* worksheet. Each group writes into large *Similarities and Differences* diagram on board or overhead. Teacher summarizes the varied attributes, directions, and styles that constitute abstract art.
4. Teacher reviews contour drawing. Teacher directs students to draw onto foam core board using black permanent marker with a pure contour or cross contour drawing of something observed (object, plant, face, hands, etc.).
5. Teacher gives a demonstration of texture rubbing with black crayon on pastel colored and white tissue paper. Students do texture rubbings on selected pastel tissue paper.
6. Teacher demonstrates adhering torn tissue paper over contour drawing on surface of foam core board using a glue wash. Students then follow with the same activity.
7. Students put their contour drawing covered with tissue paper up on board for midpoint critique. Teacher reviews attributes of abstract art and good compositional qualities with emphasis on balance and visual movement as students view their work.
8. Teacher demonstrates use of white and/or black paint to embellish tissue paper surface to enhance their abstract works of art. Give pointers on how to correct composition when embellishing surface with paint.
9. Evaluate and critique.

Fig. 4.27.

Visual Art Lesson Plan
Donna Sinicrope, Shores Acres Elementary

LESSON TITLE:
Bicycle Drawing from Real Life   Grade 2

MAIN OBJECTIVE:
Using observation and comparison to draw a bicycle from real life that is accurate in proportion and detail.

MATERIALS:
Student bicycle
9x12 white drawing paper
4B or other soft lead drawing pencil
pink erasers
markers, crayons, color pencils are optional

1. Point out the shapes and lines of the bicycle: circles, triangles, curved, straight, diagonal. Tell the students they will be drawing the bicycle as they see it so it will look real.

2. Paper is horizontal on student's desk. Draw on the board one step at a time with students. Begin by pointing to and then marking the paper halfway down on the vertical edges with pencil. Explain that this will allow for the height of the wheels and allow space for the seat and handlebars.

3. Demonstrate drawing the left tire on the left lower side of the paper. As we practice I ask "is the circle too large, is the circle too small" using a full arm motion from the shoulder down like "stirring a cake." When the circle looks just the right size, put the pencil down and draw it. We will use this size and placement for the rest of the drawing.

4. Next we draw the chain wheel. "Does it touch the back wheel? Is it larger or smaller?" Again we practice the motion of "stirring the cake" and put the pencil down to draw on the paper when the size and placement looks just right.

5. We draw the same size wheel in the right lower corner of the paper and then put a dot in the center of the three circles. We discuss radiating lines, where in the world we have seen similar lines, then draw these from the centers for spokes and chain wheel.

6. Next we draw two parallel, diagonal lines for the seat and handlebars; "which is higher?" Then the triangular seat with curved edges and curved symmetrical lines for the handlebars.

Fig. 4.27. (cont.)

7. We draw the other from bars looking at where they stop and start, one under the seat, the other at the center of the chain wheel. We then look for what is missing: wiggle the pencil around the wheel for the tires, pedals, reflectors, etc., talking about the shapes and their location.

8. Students can shade in their drawing with pencil for dark parts of the bicycle: seat, tires, handlegrips, or customize their bikes with color. Backgrounds can be added: student behind or sitting (more challenging) on the bike, a bike shop, store, parked at school or at home.

9. We hold our drawings at arm length to see if we forgot anything in the drawing, then share our drawing with each other.

VOCABULARY: **Radiating lines**   **Parallel**   **Proportion**

Critiques

Two kinds of critiques were organized following the studio workshops. One was conducted by the workshop instructors on the teachers' own creative work. The other was based on examples of student work collected by the teachers from their study class. The critique of the student work was led by the project director, the art supervisor, or by the teachers themselves. Critiques of the teachers' work. Critiques of the teachers' work were conducted by the workshop instructor Pat Priscoe, Pinellas County (Fig. 4.29) at the close of the studio sessions, where the work was either spread across the studio floor or displayed in an upright position in a hallway or gallery. The critiques generally included an analysis of the work by the workshop instructor and a dialogue with individual teachers and with the group as a whole.

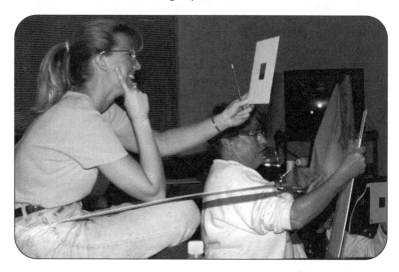

Fig. 4.28. Pinellas County art teachers using viewfinder device while drawing a still life.

Critiques of student work. Each teacher brought to the workshop four to six sample student works reflecting the lesson plan they developed at a previous studio session. These were displayed on the wall with an open discussion (see Dade County art teacher, Fig. 4.30 and Dade County art supervisor, Ray Azcuy, Fig. 4.31) following the teachers' review of the work. Generally, the discussion included an exchange of ideas on the quality of the product, the teachers' lesson plan and its implementation, and ideas teachers could offer each other on how the lesson could have been improved or reorganized to better meet the needs of students at different grade levels. These discussions among the teachers about what they were attempting to teach and how they carried it out seemed particularly rewarding to the teachers, who rarely have opportunities to share their ideas and concerns about teaching with colleagues.

Fig. 4.29. Pat Prisco, Pinellas County workshop instructor, conducting a critique of teachers' drawings.

Fig. 4.30. Dade County art teacher critiquing student work.

Summary

Chapter 4 addressed the aims of the project, the training of the teachers, the project's goals and standards, the construction of the test instruments, the scoring of student

Fig. 4.31. Ray Azcuy, Dade County Schools art supervisor, conducting a critique of student work.

portfolios, and the development of curricula. Chapter 5 will describe the field tests on electronic portfolios. The final results, recommendations, and conclusions will be presented in chapter 6 and the statistical data that support the conclusions will be presented in the Appendix.

Study Questions

1. Observe an experienced art teacher presenting a new art project to a class. Document the instructions the teacher gives orally, the visuals or examples and handouts presented, and what qualities the final product should exemplify. Create a checklist of what it is you think the teacher wants the student to know and be able to do. Observe the same events as presented by fellow art education students and contrast the expectations of both individuals.
2. Develop a lesson plan for a class based solely on achieving as many state or national standards as possible. How many of the standards were you able to use in the plan, what particular activities in the plan address each standard, and how would you evaluate whether the student achieved the standards you specified?
3. Collect a number of examples of two-dimensional artwork from a single class and separate the work into two stacks, one that contains the strongest work and the other the weakest. Describe the common visual characteristics of the work in the two stacks and then describe the visual characteristics you apparently used to divide them into the two groups. Now divide the high and low stacks into two more stacks, one high and

one low, again. Describe the visual characteristics that helped you decide the higher and lower stacks you put them in.

4. Find two or three art education texts that specify the developmental characteristics of K–2, 3–5, and 6–8 students. Select one or more of these scales and develop three elementary rubrics based on the descriptors provided in the scales. Apply these criteria to a stack of two-dimensional work that has work from all these grade levels. See if you can find the grade level of the students by using only your scale.

5. Develop a rubric or a scale that you think would accurately measure a student's achievement in art history, criticism, or aesthetics. Conduct a lesson on one of these subjects and give a test you construct to the students you have taught. Describe why you thought the test was or was not successful.

6. Using four works gathered from students in a given class, organize four sample portfolios that could be classified a 1, 2, 3, or 4 (highest). Have two other students join you and see whether they would give the same ratings to the four portfolios that you organized. Did your assessment agree or disagree with the others? If so, why?

References

Armstrong, C. L. (1994). Designing assessment in art. Reston, VA: National Art
　　　Education Association.
Askin, W. (1985). Evaluating the advanced placement portfolio in studio art.
　　　New York: The College Board
Beattie, K. B. (1997). Assessment in art education. Worcester, MA: Davis Publications
Bloom, B. (1956) in Englehart, V., Furst, E., Hill, W. and Krathwell, P. (eds.). Taxonomy of
　　　educational objectives: Handbook cognitive domain. New York: David McKay.
Dorn, C. M. (1999). Mind in art: Cognitive foundations in art education.
　　　Mahwah, NJ: Lawrence Erlbaum Associates.
Howard, V. A. (1997). Artistic practice and skills in Perkins, D. & Leondar, B. (eds.) The
　　　arts and cognition. Baltimore: John Hopkins University Press. Pages 208–240.
Lowenfeld, V. (1964). Creative and mental growth (6th edition). New York: Macmillan.
McFee, J. K. (1961). Preparation for art. San Francisco, CA: Wadsworth Publishing Co.
National Art Education Association. (1994). National visual arts standards.
　　　Reston, VA:
Piaget, J. (1952). The origins of intelligence in children, New York:
　　　International Universities Press.

5

ELECTRONIC PORTFOLIO STUDIES

Chapter 4 reported the results of the teacher training activities and the adjudication of student portfolios in Florida and Indiana. This chapter reports the efforts of four teachers in the Illinois project to use their training in assessment to help students in their classes develop their own portfolios electronically. The sample electronic portfolios presented here were developed by K–12 and college project teachers using individually designed authentic assessment strategies in their designs of the portfolios. Because they viewed their efforts more as a feasability study of the design of electronic portfolios, peer review of their assessment results were not feasible, although in their view the assessment methods used on the traditional portfolios could be used effectively on the electronic portfolios, as demonstrated in Case Study 1. Future research is still needed before the procedures documented in Chapter 4 can be used effectively in the adjudication of electronic portfolios. That research is now ongoing.

The electronic portfolio component of the Assessment of Expressive Learning Project in Illinois included four feasibility studies on the applicability of electronic portfolios as an assessment tool in the visual arts at various levels of instruction. The primary objective of the portfolio feasibility studies was to design a teacher-centered assessment technique using the art products these programs generate as the data. Further objectives were to develop a data collection system that was school based and teacher centered and that related to outcomes stated by the school for its art program. The outcomes for the program and student performance would come from selected schools that met state and national standards in the visual arts.

What this assessment design required was that the teacher and the school system take charge of the design, conceptualization, and implementation of the evaluation of the art program and student progress as discussed earlier in the text. The mechanism for collecting the data was to use the same portfolio assessment techniques that have been used in the last two decades in various forms. The unique aspect of the activity was to design a self—collecting data system where the student and the teacher could, over time, document student progress and learning using an electronic data collection system incorporating multimedia formats and design. The studies described in this chapter are based on research using electronic formats for portfolio development currently being conducted in the Division of Art Education in the School of Art at Northern Illinois University (NIU) by Professor Stanley Madeja and a group of graduate students. This chapter reports the case studies of four teachers who have developed courses of study that include using the Madeja Visual Modeling of Information System as a guideline for the construct and design of electronic portfolios. All of the K–12 case studies were conducted in schools in the greater Chicago metropolitan area. These include four selected case studies that encompass the use of electronic portfolios in elementary, high school, and university art programs. The organization and the writing of the case studies was the responsibility of the art teachers who developed the model programs. Therefore, the format for these case studies varies among the teachers, yet they have common elements derived from the Madeja Visual Modeling of Information System.

Elementary School Case Studies in Electronic Formats for Portfolio Design

Two of the feasibility studies were conducted at the elementary level at Forest Roads Elementary School in, LaGrange School District 102, LaGrange, Illinois and Spring Brook Elementary School in District 204 in Naperville, Illinois. At Forest Roads Elementary School, three classes in the sixth grade were used as the experimental groups. The total number of students was 69, the class size was 23 students per class, and their age level was 11 to 12 years old. At Spring Brook Elementary School, grade five was used with six classes. The age level was 10 to 11, with 28 students per class and a total number of 239 students participating. Both studies started in late August and ended the last day of the school year, approximately the second week in June. Two teachers, Zina McBride and Karen Popovich, conducted the classroom activities and assisted in the design of all of the programs for their schools. Over the course of the school year, six meetings were held with Stanley Madeja as part of the coordination of the project. The teachers were selected because of their previous work done at NIU with electronic portfolios. The case studies that follow describe how each site was organized and how the program was implemented. It should be noted that the two school sites used two different computer platforms: Forest Roads was Macintosh-based and Spring Brook was PC-based.

Case Study #1: Spring Brook Elementary Model

Using Electronic Portfolios in the Art Classroom to Measure and Record Student Achievement in Art by Karen Popovich, Spring Brook Elementary School, Indian Prairie School District 204, Illinois.

The use of electronic portfolios in the art classroom has proven to have many benefits for both students and teachers. An effective electronic portfolio system is developed using a combination of traditional art portfolio concepts and more modern electronic means. In this process students learn to collect, organize, manage, reflect, and evaluate their achievements in art. I have developed and implemented a system for using electronic portfolios in the art classroom to record and measure student achievement in art. This particular project was implemented at the fifth grade level, but can be easily adapted to other grade levels.

In the development of this project I focused on three main goals:

1. To design a method for using electronic portfolios as an assessment tool to measure student achievement.
2. To effectively train students to collect and manage digital images of their artwork using a digital camera.

3. To develop a system in which students can manage their own data collection system representing their art achievements through digital images and reflection writings.

Objectives for Student Learning

- Following instruction and demonstration, learners will design a portfolio out of a variety of materials and use book-binding skills. This later will be referred to as the "hard copy" of their electronic portfolio.
- Following instruction and demonstration, learners will demonstrate the ability to use a digital camera and will maintain these skills for the remainder of the school year.
- Following instruction and applicable guided practice, students will manage their digital images in a Microsoft PowerPoint slide show.
- Students each will participate in a select number of reflection activities in which they will write about their experiences with the electronic portfolio process, reflect on concepts and skills attained through the various art projects, and assess themselves using a rubric.

Benefits of Electronic Portfolios in the Art Education Classroom

There are numerous benefits of students managing their own electronic portfolios. The main benefit I observed is that such a system enables the teacher and student to assess growth over time. Each art project and periodic reflection writings are all contained in an electronic format and a small hard copy portfolio. In the reflection writings, the learners have an opportunity to reflect on their work, accomplishments, and future goals. I observed that students involved in this process took charge of their learning and had an increased level of pride and high self-esteem. In the management of their own electronic portfolios, students showed tremendous growth in organizational skills, critical thinking, and understanding of design elements. The project illustrates a clear connection between the visual art curricular goals, such as elements and principles of design, and the elementary technology curriculum.

Description of the District 204 Project

At the beginning of the school year, I discussed electronic portfolios with my students and explained the project I had developed for them. I further discussed how this was a process that they would be working on throughout the entire school year, with the culminating experience being a showing of 160 electronic portfolios at the district Fine Arts Festival. A goal that was 9 months ahead seemed unattainable, but when this project was broken down and approached in small steps, it appeared much more feasible. The first step was to design the hard copy of the portfolios that in a sense, appear to be miniportfolios measuring only about 8 in. wide and about 7 in. high. Students were taught book-binding skills to construct their portfolios and were given the freedom to design the cover using a variety of materials. A digital picture of each student was added to the front of their portfolio with their name clearly written along the top flap. The portfolios then were put away in their respective class boxes as we went on to work on our other art projects. As students were finishing their first assignment, we took time to learn how to use the digital camera and record their digital images on their own floppy disks. As each art project was completed through the school year, the students were responsible for placing their pieces of art at the photo station and recording the image on their floppy disks using the digital camera. By the beginning of October, all classes had finished the first two art projects and it was time to demonstrate Microsoft PowerPoint and give students time for guided practice with this program. I demonstrated how to set up a blank slide show, how to insert images from their floppy disks, how to edit their images, how to add and edit text, how to add a background for their slides, and how to save their Power Point presentations. A packet of Microsoft PowerPoint directions was available each time students went to a computer to update their portfolios. Students worked on this process throughout the school year and, as each slide was complete, they printed out the appropriate size and carefully mounted it in their hard-copy portfolio. Students took time periodically to complete their reflection writings in which they reflected on their comfort level with the portfolio process and on concepts and skills learned through the art projects, and completed a self-assessment of their art achievements for the grading quarter. These reflection writings provided me with some interesting insights into their thoughts and feelings about the whole process and about their achievements in art. By the time May came around, each student had 10 to 15 slides in their presentation and had gained a comfort level with the digital camera and with the slide show program. Students were given an opportunity to add transitions, timings, and sound to their slide shows before they were all looped together and recorded for showing at the district's Fine Arts Festival in May.

Assessment Component

At the end of each grading quarter, I utilized these portfolios as a way to assess each student's achievement in art. In evaluating approximately 160 fifth-grade students and more than 600 other students each quarter, I found this process to be a time saver in the end. All evidence of student achievement was contained in both a 3.5-in. floppy disk and an 8-in. hard-copy portfolio. These small versions held a digital representation of two-dimensional and three-dimensional projects and reflection writings. I used a rubric to evaluate the body of work done over the given time period. Each portfolio was assessed on a 6-point scale. I looked specifically at the effective use of elements and principles of design, craftsmanship and skill, creative and original ideas, and the overall organization of the portfolio.

Self-Assessment

I feel it is very important to reflect on ways to further improve this project. Because this project was ongoing over the entire school year, many adjustments were made through the year, such as saving the PowerPoint presentations to the school server instead of to a second disk. Many students found it difficult to distinguish between the disk used in the digital camera and the disk used to save the presentation. Another way to improve this project in the future would be to incorporate sketchbook assignments into the hard copy of the portfolios. In another year, I also may have students participate in peer reflections to gain a better understanding of how artwork is judged and to provide constructive criticism.

My fifth-grade students were challenged with this project, but they all stepped up to this challenge and came up with some very professional electronic portfolios. The students are very proud of these portfolios; one of the most difficult elements of the process was convincing them to keep the portfolios in the art room until the end of the school year. Photographing their artwork and managing their portfolios became second nature as it became part of the everyday routine in art class. One student wrote in his portfolio, "I think this portfolio will help me get a job some day." When thinking about this, I realized he was not too far off. He wouldn't exactly be taking this fifth-grade electronic portfolio with him to a job interview, but rather his increased level of organizational skills, knowledge and understanding of the elements and principles of design, and the ability to manage his own data collection system with examples of his art works that illustrate achievement in art.

Visual Art State Goals and Learning Standards Achieved Through Electronic Portfolios

- State Goal 25: Know the language of the arts.
    -Learning Standard A: Understand the sensory elements, organizational principles and expressive qualities in the arts.
    -Learning Standard B: Understand similarities, distinctions in and among the arts.
- State Goal 26: Through creating and performing, understand how works of art are produced.
    -Learning Standard A: Understand processes, traditional tools, and modern technologies used in the arts.
    -Learning Standard B: Apply skills and knowledge necessary to create and perform in the arts.
- State Goal 27: Understand the role of arts in civilization, past and present.
    -Learning Standard A: Analyze how the arts function in history, society, and everyday life.
    -Learning Standard B: Analyze how the arts shape or influence and reflect history, society, and everyday life.

National Content Standards Covered Through This Electronic Portfolio Process

1. Understanding and applying media, techniques, and processes.
2. Using knowledge of structure and functions.
3. Choosing and evaluating a range of subject matter, symbols, and ideas.
4. Reflecting upon and assessing the characteristics and merits of their work and works of others.
5. Making connections between the visual arts and other disciplines.

District 204 Visual Art Curriculum Standards Achieved Through Electronic Portfolios

- Demonstrate an understanding of the design principles to create works of art. (Content Standard 2, Achievement Standard D)
- Examine the subject matter in a personal work of art. (Content Standard 5, Achievement Standard A)
- Describe a personal work of art. (Content Standard 5, Achievement Standard B)
- Analyze a personal work of art. (Content Standard 5, Achievement Standard C)
- Interpret what is happening in a personal work of art. (Content Standard 5, Achievement Standard D)
- Express an opinion regarding a personal work of art. (Content Standard 5, Achievement Standard E)
- Create a slide show presentation.
- Add and import sounds to a slide show presentation.
- Create a hypermedia presentation to include three or more slides and three or more linked media components (sound, animation, text, graphics, etc.). Become aware of the value and applications of electronic communication.
- Know the difference between and be able to use SAVE and SAVE AS.
- Develop window skills (change size, scroll, make active, move, close).
- Select and access a printer on the network.
- Organize and save documents in folders (create, name, and rename folders).
- Diskette skills: Initialize, copy files to and from.
- Identify and learn appropriate use of physical components of a computer system.
- Demonstrate competency and safe use of a computer (start up, shut down, etc.).
- Use appropriate software and hardware independently and collaboratively to support learning across the curriculum.
- Learn the purpose and value of technology equipment.
- Operate a variety of equipment (e.g., digital camera).
- Select and apply menu commands.
- Open and Close a program.
- Recognize and apply the function of the tool icons.

- Create, name, and save a new document to disk or server.
- Open an existing document.
- Text: Select, insert, move, delete, copy, cut, and paste.
- Scroll through a document.
- Format characters: font size, color, style.
- Locate and insert graphics: delete, crop, flip, resize, rotate, move.
- Create a hypermedia presentation to include three or more slides and three or more linked media components (sound, animation, text, graphics, etc.).
- Become aware of the value and applications of electronic communication.
- Apply zoom control.
- Save changes early and often.
- Print a document.
- Create a product that uses data collected from a variety of sources.
- Add transitions to a slide show.

Case Study #2: Forest Roads Elementary Model

Inspire students with the excitement and challenge of trying something new. Yes, new challenges and ideas can be a little frightening, unsettling, and difficult to understand and implement. In the end, isn't this what we want for our educational system? Education does focus on past human experience, where we come from, how our world has developed and even present-day issues. I think it also includes the goal of implementing our new technology. The rate of speed that puts technology into our lives has increased like no other period in the past. This, coupled with the fact the world is based on visual images, makes it even more important that, as teachers, we learn and pass on this new technology. We must remain open and experiment with these new tools, so we can control the direction of our world. What holds most people back is fear of change and fear of the unknown. I am definitely part of this group, but when forced to jump in, I tread to keep my head above water. Treading can lead to floating, which can lead to swimming. This is just what happened to me. I have learned to swim in technology. I am not a great swimmer, but I can hold my head up and I get better every day. I got a taste of technology in graduate school and liked what it offered. It was difficult and frustrating at times, but it provided so many possibilities that I withstood the frustration. I realized early on that, when obstacles arose, you looked for someone much younger than yourself to help with computer problems. Today's students are growing up with technology and they can perform comfortably with many computer applications.

During a graduate class last summer, I focused my research on technology and became very interested in electronic portfolios. I decided that, when the next school year began, I was going to try using electronic portfolios with my students. Fortunately, I was asked to participate in the research program conducted by Stan

Madeja, Charles Dorn, and Robert Sabol dealing with this topic. I was grateful for the opportunity and for knowing I would have the support of other people concerned with technology issues.

Getting Started

I am employed in a school district that has a strong focus on technology, so the equipment I needed was available. Planning was the first priority, so after researching what other schools had done and considering my own use of a presentation program for introducing new lessons, I decided that students could use a Claris slide show format to present their artwork. At our school, students are familiar with Claris slide shows, having used them in other classes. I considered the equipment and began by creating a layout of the room to provide for the project. The art room has one digital camera and a tripod was borrowed from the library. An easel was used to display work for photographing. Our school policy is four students per computer, so there are four ibooks and four older computers with disk access and two disks per student, one for their images and one to be used for saving their portfolio. The disks hold 1.44MB and the portfolios are at 4.44MB. Thinking ahead, I would have students bring a zip disk at the end of the year. I presented this problem to our tech person who would burn CDs for each student if they supplied the disks. I am planning to buy the CDs in bulk and students can pay me at cost for a CD if they want a copy of their portfolio. Also, creation of files on our school server for storing all the portfolios by class, so students and teachers can access the work.

Benefits of the Electronic Portfolio as an Assessment Tool

Students are self-directed. Once students learned how to use the equipment and felt comfortable, the atmosphere in the classroom changed considerably. Students worked on multiple projects, making art, photographing, formatting the portfolio, and insetting images. There was energy, activity, and a sense of empowerment in the classroom. Students had a sense of pride in their work. Knowing that their art was being put into the presentation program made each assignment more important to them. There was a greater sense of ownership, they were spending more time on each assignment, and they understood that what they were making (the portfolio) would be a permanent record. Students were reflecting more on their progress. After working on their art and completing each project, they worked with the digital images. They manipulated and organized these images into their portfolios, which gave them another opportunity to reflect on the finished product. I had them include a reflection page in the portfolios, which allowed for written assessment on the year's work. In the future, I would add a reflection page after each trimester.

The Importance of Visual Presentations and Electronic Formats

Students had to consider composition and appearance. Through trial and error, they were making decisions about their presentations. They were learning how to get their messages to the viewer. Students were learning a marketable skill and planning for their future. With a Student Statement Card students could write a personal statement to the viewer regarding what they had learned or felt they had accomplished with the project. Colleges are having students use electronic portfolios to present material for evaluation. Businesses and people in the work force are using presentation programs to deliver information. Students working with these portfolios were gaining knowledge to prepare them for future technology challenges. Teachers can assess student growth by having student work presented in this format, which allows educators to look at an entire year or multiple years' work in evaluating progress. Storage and handling of artwork in electronic formats meant that less room was needed for storing art projects and that evaluating and grading the artwork could be done away from school.

Promoting the Art Program

The project has validated the art program in our school and the district. In a recent art show at our local library, I placed a laptop computer into a glass display case and it continuously showed 13 electronic portfolios created by the students. The positive response from other art teachers, parents, and visitors was overwhelming. I have been asked to present an overview of the project to the school board. Teachers have asked for information about the implementation of the project and another teacher in our school is planning a similar project with her second-grade students. Technology has been added to the art curriculum and new equipment has been ordered.

The Future, Next Steps

Will I do this again? Absolutely! I am now planning to start in the fourth grade with digital imagery. Fifth grade will do the same and learn to manipulate their images. Sixth grade will create an electronic portfolio next year with more reflection. Assessment of student work will be done three or four times during the school year, based on the schools grading periods of either trimesters (3) or quarters (4). A model based on trimester grading would be:

- First grading period.
- Approximately 9 weeks.
- Expected to have three to four art projects completed.
- Graded on a 4-point scale using the provided assessment model.
- Work will be assessed by the two art teachers (the instructor for the projects and another art teacher).

- Second grading period:
- Approximately 13 weeks.
- Expected to have three to four art projects completed.
- Graded on a 4-point scale using the provided assessment mode.
- Work will be assessed by the instructor for the projects.
- This assessment will be based strictly on the current body of work.
- Third grading period:
- Approximately 13 weeks.
- Expected to have three to four art projects completed.
- Graded on a 4-point scale using the provided assessment model.
- Works will be assessed holistically, using all works from the second and third grading periods, but excluding the base-line assessment from the first grading period.
- Work will be assessed by the two art teachers (the instructor for the projects and another art teacher).
- Assessment done on quarter grading periods would follow the same format as for trimesters, but would insert a duplicate of the second grading period as their third quarter and then:
- Finish the assessment process for the fourth quarter as third grading period.

Hardware And Environment Needs For Project

Figure 5.1 projects minimal and ideal needs for completing an electronic portfolio. These needs are based on my work, implementing this assignment with elementary students. Class size for this study was approximately 25 students, including some with special needs. In the district where this project took place, Apple computers are used and there are no computer labs. The school policy is a ratio of four students to each computer. Because my largest class size is 31, I have three computers with A drives and five I books. Though this assignment is based on individual work, it also affords many opportunities for collaborative work with small groups.

Fig 5.1.

HARDWARE	MINIMAL NEEDS	IDEAL NEEDS
Computers	Four: If there is a computer lab, students can leave the art room individually or as a class.	A ratio of 4 to 1 is ideal. Students stay in the art room and work at their own pace. Computers are equipped with a beaming capacity, thus eliminating cords.
Disks	Two: one for images and one for the electronic portfolio	Two: with extra disks available
Disk containers	One for each class	Two: one for disks holding images and one for the electronic portfolio
Digital camera	One: Students use the camera when an assignment is completed. No more than two students at the camera at one time.	Two cameras and extra batteries. A camera with an AC adapter would be ideal.
Tripod	None	One or more depending on the number of cameras
Easel	None	One or more depending on the sites for photography
Internal network	None: All work is saved to a disk and possibly stored on desktop folders with student names.	If the school has a network, all information held on the disks should also be saved in students' folders on the network.
Audio monitor	If there is no means for visual display, printed information must be produced for tutorials of the project.	A single monitor or other visual display equipment enables tutorial to be viewed by the entire class
Presentation Program	Claris or MS PowerPoint	Multiple programs

Fig 5.1. (cont.)

ENVIRONMENT	MINIMAL NEEDS	IDEAL NEEDS
Classroom	In smaller space, careful consideration to organization and layout is essential. Computers should be placed far enough apart to allow small groups to work uninterrupted.	Enough space to allow studio work and the placement of computers in low traffic areas
Computer access	Placement of computers in low traffic areas with consideration to electrical outlets. Two to three students can work collaboratively with the computer.	Placement of computers in low-traffic areas with the use of hubs when multiple computers are used. Students can work individually or in small groups (two).
Photography station	One: with a backdrop or easel to present work to photograph	Two: with backdrop or easel to present work, additional lighting sources
Storage	Containers for disks and artwork	Individual storage for each student's disks and artwork
Printed materials	Handouts allow additional means of instruction and reference for students.	Handouts allow additional means of instruction and reference for students.

Fig 5.2. Sample Portfolio by Sarah

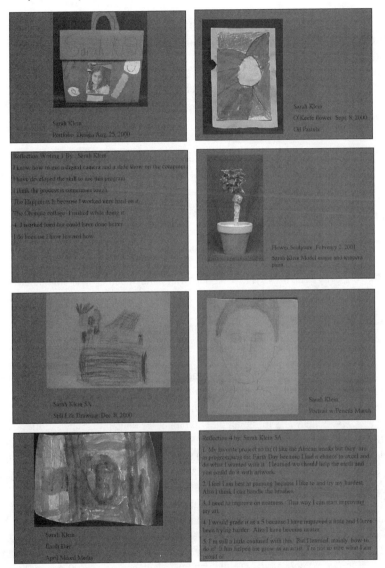

High School Case Studies in Electronic Formats for Portfolio Design

The feasibility studies at the high school level were conducted by high school art teachers who had an interest in investigating the use of electronic portfolios as part of their assessment process. The group was a subset of the 20 teachers who participated in the quantification of artworks in the high school level described in Chapter 4. The study is ongoing and Debra Fitzsimmons' case study describes the work she conducted in the academic year 2000–2001 in applying electronic formats to high school portfolios.

Case Study #3: The Mundelein High School Model

The High School Studies in Electronic Formats, Debra Fitzsimmons, Mundelein High School, Mundelein, Illinois

I first introduced the electronic portfolio into my AP seminar class. This class meets for the entire year. I chose this group for the following reasons:

1. The class size was 24. These students had the most to gain immediately from constructing a digital portfolio. They could use it for job, college, or scholarship applications.

2. They were our most advanced students. It seemed more reasonable to work out the process with a group that would be most capable of identifying these problems from a student perspective.

My plan was to first identify a program for the construction of student-created digital portfolios, and then to construct a template for student portfolio creation. The really important element was that students be able to create the portfolios themselves.

Additionally, there is ample empirical evidence to suggest that student learning, self-reflection, and goal setting are increased through the self-creation and maintenance of portfolios. I chose to use a specific slide presentation software program for several reasons. It needed to be a user-friendly program. It needed to allow for multiple frames to be viewed at one time. It needed to be easy to present the portfolio to the student and myself on the screen, but also to show the portfolio to the whole class with a projector. It needed to allow for documentation of size and media and it also would have to allow for students' written reflections and analysis. The last criterion was that it be affordable. I investigated many programs but chose one that was already included in our school software "suite" and was installed on all 700 computers in our building. Our school has a LAN and provides each student with an account on the fileserver. They can access their accounts from any school computer. This was helpful because most general classrooms are assigned only one computer. I was able to get a second, older computer around mid-year, but, of course, a project like this requires that students have more access. Our school places the vast majority of computers in the Learning Resource Center and in five large computer labs located throughout the building. By building on the fileserver account, the students were able to go to a lab and work, but they could also access what they had done on the classroom computer.

Instead of developing an instructional handbook, I developed a template. The template was constructed to give a child without previous knowledge of the program an easy start, but still allowing for creativity for the more technically advanced student. Students were told that they had the freedom to develop the portfolio as they wished and that the template was only there to get them started. The program allowed for the customizing of visual information through its many graphic features. The template was built to match the students' needs within the context of the Mundelein High School AP Studio Art curriculum goals. In January, I took the entire class to a lab. They all had disks with digital images of their first-semester work. The digital images came either from the students using the digital camera to document their work or from a slide scanned to get the JPEG. The students had the option to scan their own slides or to have the scanning done at a photo shop. Our local shop charged the AP art students a very inexpensive rate for this service. The first thing that they learned was how to clean up their images in a visual editing program. There really was not much to learn. Our purpose was to use features that would maintain the fidelity of the original work. Once the Rotate, Crop, and Balance commands were mastered, we went right to the template. Six of the students were already fluent with the program and became my assistants. The kids simply went through the template. They learned to insert text, to insert and size their images, and to insert or delete slides. They also learned how to change the view from full screen to thumbnails. It was a learning revelation for them because they could see all of their work together. About 4 weeks before the end of the school year, we returned to the lab to customize the portfolios.

Most of the students had already discovered the options. My strongest insistence was that the frills should never detract from the presentation of their work and their ideas, and that the file's size not exceed the system's ability to hold it. We had no Zip drives or CD burners. Some students did go beyond the capacity of the 3.5-in. disks. Two students compressed theirs into HTML format. During the time of their construction, I began to see development in reflection and in their ability to go back and improve their work due to this reflection. The electronic portfolio seemed to give them something that I had only seen in my own work as an adult at my first one-person show. There is an idea that runs throughout the things that we do. Sometimes it takes stepping back to see it. The portfolios allowed the students to be able to do this. Because this trial was going so well, my colleagues and I developed a template for the Art I students. This template was to be a weekly recording of their work. It included a slide for images, a slide for reflection, and a slide with a simple self-evaluation. I introduced it the first week of the term. Students were given simple instructions on how to use the digital cameras and again we went up to the lab as a group to learn the basics. This group was amazing. They were very excited about documenting their work. I had them work in teams of two or three. In these groups, the students developed their own routines that included informal critiques and assistance in the process. One of the things that we found right away was that the once-a-week documentation was not the right fit for this curriculum: It was just too much documentation. It did not correspond to the stages of the projects that they were in. Therefore, I changed it so that they could record their work at the conclusion of every unit. That was good because no two students ever finished the unit at the same time and those who were ahead could document. Those who were in the middle could document in a group with the help of the advanced students and those who were a little slower could use resource time.

I began the term by using the traditional way of grading, but, as we approached midterm, I asked the students to turn in their disks. I wanted to review them because I thought it might be beneficial to use them at midterm grading. What I found was that the students' process and products were right before my eyes. In the structure, I asked that they document some process work and that they include a reflection for each piece. But they chose what that would be. I also required that they put in the finished pieces for each assignment. We only have 8 weeks and that, at best, means four to five finished pieces in the survey classes. Those works are important

Fig. 5.3. Sample Portfolio Advanced Placement concentration, Mario (Selections)

5 ELECTRONIC PORTFOLIO STUDIES

Fig. 5.3. Sample Portfolio Advanced Placement concentration, Mario (Selections) (cont.)

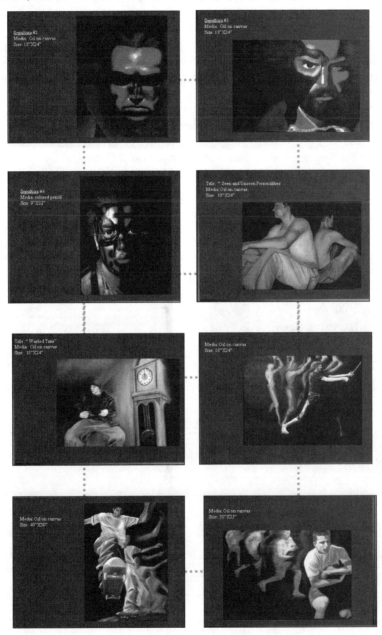

demonstrations of how students are learning and are important in a term portfolio. I have found that students get excited when they have completed a piece and they are ready to document: It is like the pronouncement of accomplishment. I have found the written reflection to be more beneficial than I had originally anticipated. I required students to address the lesson criteria in the reflection and to include their thoughts about their learning in each unit, with the purpose of reinforcing the visual learning. What I got was a window into their thoughts that I had not received before. As a teacher, it is my goal to work and discuss work with each child daily, but that is not always the reality. Even when it is, mathematically we could only have 4 minutes of one-on-one discussion so, the reflections are helping me to get to know the students better. I also believe that they help the children to better think about their work.

Fig. 5.4. Sample Portfolio Drawing I Mathew, (selections)

Fig. 5.4. Sample Portfolio Drawing I Mathew, (selections) (cont.)

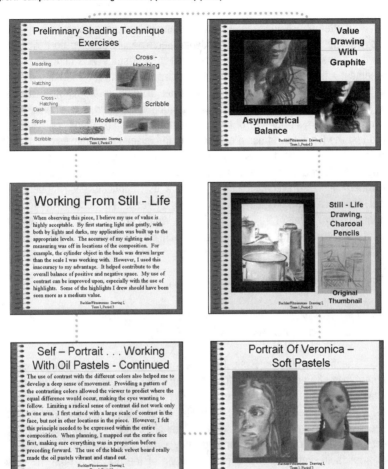

5 ELECTRONIC PORTFOLIO STUDIES

University Studies in Electronic Formats for Portfolio Design

An attempt was made to also use existing entry-level art classes in the studio area to test the feasibility of having students electronically develop portfolios of the assigned artwork for a drawing and design class. This study was conducted over a three-semester time frame that started in the spring semester of 2000 and continued in the fall of that year and in the spring semester of 2001. In the spring semester of 2000, Professor Shei-Chou Wang, a doctoral student, selected a beginning drawing class for a pilot study on the use of the Madeja model. This first semester actually was used to test the feasibility of using electronic data collection techniques and how they might be integrated into the assessment of student learning into a semester-long drawing class. After a pilot study was completed, a strategy was developed which used the Northern Illinois University Ethernet network that connects each student to the internet. This solved the problems of visual data's storage and became the format for the management system use by Professor Wang in the next two semesters. Approximately 40 students each semester participated in the study. What follows are examples of courses of study and one portfolio.

Case Study #4: The Northern Illinois University Model

The Use of the Madeja Visual Modeling of Information System in Beginning College Drawing Courses by Shei-Chou Wang, Northern Illinois University

The final project in Basic Drawing I is the conceptualization, design, and implementation of an electronic portfolio. The portfolio is based on work students have accumulated during the semester. The students are alerted to this project early on in the semester. As the course progresses, they digitally record their work and then are asked to select two pieces from each problem for a total of 10 pieces that will be used as the subject matter and content for the portfolio. They also can supplement the portfolio with works from their sketchbooks if applicable. Each of the drawings from the class is recorded by a digital camera and stored on a disk. From this set of drawings and designs, they are asked to create a PowerPoint presentation that includes all the images, plus analysis and interpretation of these images, explanation of the technical and artistic qualities, and the students' artistic intent statement. The electronic portfolio acts as a part of the final exam for the drawing and design courses. It is also a visual record of the students' accomplishments over the semester time frame and provides additional evidence for the students' understanding of the content in each problem. The students also create a web page. The web page acts as a record of their accomplishments in the course, including the portfolio. The student can create the page with as much additional information as they deem necessary to demonstrate what they have learned. What follows is a sample course design for the drawing and design classes taught and developed by Shei-Chou Wang at Northern Illinois University, School of Art. In addition, a description of the final exam for the course shows how the electronic portfolio relates to the other requirements. The storyboards at the end of this section provide a visual outline of the electronic portfolios each student created to meet the course requirements.

Art 100 Basic Drawing

1. Nature of the Course
Introduction to drawing. Emphasis on object representation through description and expressive means. Control of line, value and spatial illusion with a variety of media.
2. Objectives
This course is designed for the beginning art student with an emphasis in drawing. The class will be structured around exploring various drawing media and techniques while drawing from observation and imagination. Both traditional and nontraditional drawing formats and concepts will be introduced to students in order to broaden their vision in the arts. Students will present their talents through drawing and share the diverse outcomes with their peers. Throughout the semester, students will be able to develop knowledge in arts and art language, improve drawing skills, and appreciate broad art styles; furthermore, they will carry a positive attitude to contribute their life in art in the future.
3. Textbook
Enstice, Wayne & Peters, Melody, Drawing: Space, Form & Expression, 2nd Edition, Prentice Hall, Inc., 1996.

4. Assignments
4.1 The Use of the Electronic Media:
  • Learning Microsoft Word, PowerPoint and scanning under the PC (IBM) environment.
  • E-mail: students must send a testing mail to the instructor before September 1. It is the fastest way to communicate with the classmates and instructor.
  • Web Board: students have to login in the web board and learn to use the basic functions (Details will be given later). This is the place to check upcoming assignments, post the written and research assignments, and receive supporting information.
  • PowerPoint Portfolio: students will be asked to create a 15-page electronic portfolio by using MS PowerPoint.
4.2 Visual Resources:
  • Students are required to collect journal-type information and references relating to the topics in order to enrich their resource bank.
4.3 Art Event Participation:
  • Students are required to attend five or more arts events during the semester. The events can be exhibitions in Northern Illinois University Jack Olson Gallery, Chicago museums and galleries, concerts, plays, or dance performances. Tickets or program flyers can be proof of your attendance.

4.4 Five Topics (individual handouts):
- These five topics are designed to have students apply the knowledge of drawing technically and artistically. Each assignment is a unit to help students build up a complete picture of drawing.

4.5 Writing Exercises:
- Each topic has several questions; students need to put their own words together to answer. These exercises provide the opportunity for students to write and think in many different ways relating to aesthetic and history issues that they have never done before.

4.6 Tests:
- Five tests will be given during the semester. The purpose is to examine students' understanding of the concepts and further to challenge them to establish their knowledge of each concept for future use.

4.7 Final Project:
- Beginning Drawing I Portfolio: a portfolio is a student's summary of this course, which shows skills, images, and ideas he/she has learned and created.
- Electronic Portfolio (stated above).
- Artist's Book: a comprehensive activity combining research, creativity and communication prepares students to move forward to the higher level of studies.

5. Grading:
- There is no reason not to give hard-working students a golden "A" unless a student 1) misses classes, 2) delays assignments, 3) shows little or no effort on given assignments, and 4) expresses bad behavior.
- Attending this course is not only for a grade but also is a process to help students grow in many aspects as a complete foundation; furthermore, students will be able to use this foundation and accomplish their future success.
- The measurement of student's performance includes five perspectives, which cover the evaluation of a student's development of knowledge, skills, imagination, creativity, confidence, patience, and enjoyment of making art in a semester period.

5 ELECTRONIC PORTFOLIO STUDIES

Grade Reference A: 501–600, B: 451–500, C: 426–450,D: 401–425, F: 400 and below

Perspective	Points	Contents	Assessment
Qualitative Merit	100	• Creativity	• 20 points on each topic
		• Originality	• Looking for the overall value of each topic (include all exercises and practices).
		• Effort	• Minor mistakes or one bad (ugly) piece will not affect the overall value.
		• Presentation (Techniques, Neatness)	
		• Meaningfulness (Concepts)	
		• Meeting the requirements and beyond	
Quantitative Merit	100	• The amount of assignment (homework and in-class works)	• 20 points on each topic • Unlimited delay reduction
		• On time/Delay	
		• Redoing or extra works	• 3 points for each extra work
Scholarly Merit	150	• Written assignment	• 10 points on each topic
		• Research and project preparation	• 10 points on each test
		• Tests	• 25 points on the event participation
		• Web board participation	• 25 points on remaining
		• Arts events participation	
Self-Evaluation	100	• Self-evaluation	• 30 points on each self-evaluation
		• Peer review	• Extra point opportunity from peer review; no reduction from peer review
		• Attendance	• Unlimited reduction for lateness and absence
Developmental Evaluation	150	• Final Project	• 100 points electronic portfolio, and 50 points artist book)
		• Monthly Review	• 10 points on each review
		• Attitude and progress	

Fig. 5.5. Sample Portfolio, The e-Portfolio, Nathan (selections)

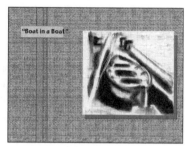

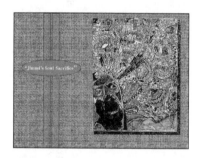

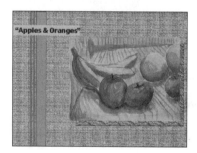

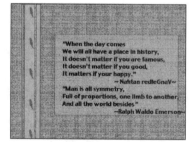

Application of The Electronic Portfolio to Evaluation Of Expressive Learning

The case studies reported in this chapter illustrate how electronic portfolios can be integrated into the curriculum and act as a visual-verbal record of student expressive learning. In the elementary case studies, the procedures for the evaluation of student work, as described in Chapter 2, was used as a mechanism for grading the student's art works for each grading period. The portfolio became a culminating experience as suggested in the Madeja Visual Modeling of Information System. The Portfolio was used effectively in each grading period to document the letter grade. It acted as a record of the student's accomplishments and made the criteria used for grading clear to the parents and the student.

At the high school level the electronic portfolios can be used as a visual record of the students' accomplishments over a semester and to document visual presentation techniques the student uses to organize the knowledge base for the course of study. Further, it can be used by the teacher to explain to the parents what the student has accomplished, becoming part of the basis for determining the final grade of the portfolio, and it forms a visual record of a body of work that could be used professionally for college admissions or used as a professional portfolio for someone seeking employment. It is anticipated that portfolio development would start at the beginning of the students' high school program and continue over the students' high school program of study. This would also provide a comprehensive record of the students' accomplishment in the visual arts for two to three years. At Mundelein High School, the portfolio was used in an Advanced Placement Program format where students had the option create an electronic portfolio of their work using the AP format to supplement the original works.

At the university level the portfolio was used as a website, and was only part of the assessment process used for evaluation of the student. However, it became the culminating activity for students in a beginning course and their first visual record of the artistic quality of their drawings. It also demonstrated the students' ability to use electronic media as a presentation technique in the visual modeling of information.

Study Questions

1. Using the examples described in Chapters 2 and 5, select one of the formats such as a portfolio/journal and define a time frame and problem. Find a class at a level to which you have access, elementary, secondary, or at the college level, and work with a student(s) in this class, teaching them how to develop an electronic portfolio as described in this text. Replicate or design your own study that utilizes the electronic portfolio as a technique for assessing expressive learning. Develop a context for using a portfolio in the overall assessment of a course of study.
2. Create your own electronic portfolio outlining your own work as a visual presentation using PowerPoint and the Madeja Visual Modeling Of Information System as a guide.

This portfolio should be considered as a record of your scholarly and artistic production providing not only images of your work but also an analysis and interpretation about what you're trying to express. You may comment on the artistic intent of your work as well as on the studio processes and techniques that contributes to the work's expressive and aesthetic qualities. The time frame, as indicated in the description of the model, will be determined by the user.

3. Develop an archival record of your visual accomplishments, which can be used as a visual database. This will become a record of your artwork stored in a common file format such as jpeg, which can be used to create an electronic portfolio and/or other visual presentations of both your studio and scholarly efforts.

6

CONCLUSIONS AND RECOMMENDATIONS

Chapter 6 reports the conclusions and recommendations for each of the study's three investigations: (a) the assessment of student art portfolios; (b) the assessment concerns of teachers, students, and artists; and (c) the future possibilities for using student-developed electronic portfolios as a way to document student progress in K–12 art schooling.

This project represented a unique collaborative effort among three major higher education research institutions in a partnership with K–12 public school art teachers in the field. In addition, this effort produced substantially increased interactions among art education faculty in these institutions. It also led to the sharing of multiple viewpoints and philosophies while stimulating the development of the project. The collaboration among higher education faculty also fostered a mixture of knowledge and expertise among individuals to produce an even broader perspective with which to identify and resolve research questions and approaching issues related to art assessment. This higher education collaboration also contributed to the translation of these inputs from art teachers into the ways we conduct the preservice assessment training of art teachers.

The collaboration of researchers from higher education with art teachers from the field also provided a unique opportunity for matching accepted research methodologies and practices with the identified needs of art teachers. The blending of common interests and needs provided benefits to both groups. Findings from the studies suggest that there is a marked need for members of the higher education community to conduct school-based research with practical applications. The research and involvement of the higher education community with art teachers and schools offers the potential to improve art education in ways that other kinds of research may not. This research also contributes to the researchers' understanding of issues and concerns that are of importance to practitioners. By shaping research goals based on this kind of activity, researchers can provide better information and more assistance in resolving the problems faced by practitioners. The practical value of this research will further benefit the research community by identifying additional issues and research questions of a philosophical and theoretical nature.

Outcomes from this project support the need for more school-based research involving collaborations between the higher education community and art teachers in the field. Additional studies of assessment and its implications for the field of art education are necessary. These studies, whether quantitative or qualitative, also should investigate the effects assessment has had on the field. Future studies also should include the impact of assessment on curriculum, instruction, and the quality of student work. Empirical studies of student achievement in art education like those conducted in this project can help provide a foundation for understanding the impact of assessment on learning in the field.

Results of the Student Portfolio Assessment

As previously noted, the project was not designed as an experimental study involving experimental and control groups. Therefore, some of the conclusions must be considered as tentative, requiring further investigation. The principal study question as to whether the assessment process was itself reliable was confirmed based on the study sample that included 51 classrooms and nearly 1,000 students. Some of the other conclusions, including the influence of the in-service studio and curriculum training on student performances at different levels, at different sites, and on students at different grade levels, require further study.

What also should be kept in mind is that the study participants did not constitute a random sample population, but rather were volunteers from 51 different schools and 15 different school districts, each operating in a different context with different school populations and with differing resources and school support levels. Although comparisons between schools and between students were necessary in order to confirm the effectiveness of the assessment process, these comparisons do not support the goals of authentic assessment, which is not designed to compare teachers and schools with one another, but rather to assess student progress within a given classroom as a guide to improving the quality of instruction.

Results of the study indicate the following:

1. The analysis of the data derived from the adjudication of nearly 2,000 portfolios and 16,000 student artworks confirms that an authentic assessment process where art teachers are trained how to conduct themselves will produce quantifiable and reliable estimates of student performance in the making of expressive objects. Additionally, these results suggest that qualitative instructional outcomes can be assessed quantitatively, yielding score values that can be manipulated statistically and that produce measures that are both valid and reliable estimates of student art performance.

2. This adjudication process involving art teachers and their students clearly demonstrates that art teachers with appropriate training can govern themselves and set their own standards for providing valid and reliable estimates of their own students' performances. It further demonstrates that these performances reflect the values of the teacher, the student, the school program, and the goals of learning in art.

3. The study data further support the notion that the project rubrics employed in these authentic assessment settings by teachers familiar with the nature of creative forming in art can lead to the assessment process that effectively measures student expressive outcomes, guided only by developmentally ordered rubrics and the teachers' own intuitive knowledge of artistic thinking and making. These results suggest, more importantly,

that there are viable alternatives to paper-and-pencil tests in art assessment, that teacher bias can even be a positive force in assessing art products, and that all art teachers need not be expected to teach and all students need not perform in the same way.

4. The analysis of the data suggests that differences in student art performance and their progress will vary among different classrooms, at different grade levels, and in different school districts. These findings suggest that student and teacher abilities and school environments are unequally distributed and that comparisons made among the performances of teachers, students, schools, and school districts are neither useful nor compatible with the goals of improving instruction. A competitively ordered assessment of the performances of teachers and students in different schools and in different school districts is both inappropriate and counterproductive to achieving the aims of authentic school assessment.

5. The analysis of the data on the question of whether student expressive performances improved over time suggests, but does not empirically confirm, that gains in student performance may be related in a positive way to the teacher workshop interventions, the grade level of the student, and the student's expressive abilities. Overall, student performance gains were unevenly distributed among different grade levels, among teachers receiving the same or different studio training, and among students of unequal expressive ability. These data, which support the idea that the students of teachers who received no training (Illinois) made less progress than the students of teachers who received the training, suggest that the inservice training of the teacher has a positive effect on student performance. Some results (Indiana) also suggest that teachers receiving the same training may not equally benefit the performance of the student. This raises questions about both the quality and amount of training and how useful it is to the teachers who received it.

The Study of Student, Teacher, and Artist Behavior

Findings in the research study on art teachers, students of art, and artists conducted as part of the project, as reported in Chapter 5, raise assessment issues and concerns for future research in the field of art education. It must be kept in mind that these studies were conducted with small samples and generalizations about the findings must be cautious. However, many findings from this study are compatible with findings from previous studies by Sabol (1994, 1998a, 1998b, 1999, 2001) and Sabol and Bensur (2000) involving significantly larger populations of art teachers that have produced generalizations useful to the field. In order to further generalize these findings, they need to be replicated with larger samples. Additional recommendations for future research will be presented later in this chapter.

6 CONCLUSIONS AND RECOMMENDATIONS

The results reveal that three fourths of the art teachers had received some assessment training in college courses, 80% had gained assessment knowledge and experience through on-the-job experience, and 78% cited interaction with colleagues as their principal means of assessment information and training. These findings are significant in that they suggest a need for more in-depth assessment training in preservice preparation programs and also for in-service and professional development programming for art teachers in the field. Assessment training for preservice art teachers and practitioners that provides opportunities for professional development can be offered in the form of school district in-service training, graduate courses, state art education association workshops, recertification programs, and license renewal credits. Art teachers should voice their needs for assessment training and seek opportunities to acquire it. A long-term commitment to providing professional development opportunities must be made by local school districts, institutions of higher education, state art education associations, and state departments of education in order to meet this need.

Although, as a group, the art teachers in the project felt they had adequate training in assessment findings from the study suggest that preservice training of art teachers in assessment is inadequate. Art teachers need in-depth training in assessment methods as evidenced in their open-ended responses on questionnaires.

Study findings on art teacher attitudes toward assessment supported the findings of other studies by Sabol (1994, 1998a, 1998b, 1999, 2001) and Sabol and Bensur (2000). These studies also suggest that art teachers support assessment in art education and that art teachers are fully aware of the potential drawbacks associated with assessment. In the open-ended responses and in the discussions at the workshop sessions, art teachers felt they needed to embrace assessment and become proactive in supporting it. They also suggested a need to develop and continuously refine assessment processes that really work within the school setting. Many art teachers bemoaned the fact that some art teachers tend to view assessment negatively or conduct it with suspicion. Rather than seeing assessment as a distraction, the teachers suggested that assessment could be a powerful ally in promoting the program. They felt that, with further training, they could educate administrators and the public about the art learning and levels of student achievement in their programs. In their view, administrators too often failed to see the importance and relevance of assessment in art education programs. They also recommended that assessment results be used to report student achievement levels to stakeholders and provide evidence of the students' achievement in the works their students produce. It further was suggested that assessment results were an essential leveraging tool, capable of influencing decisions that directly or indirectly effect art education programs, and that the results could be used to track and demonstrate student, class, and program achievements over time. Assessment results also should be used to identify what the curriculum is and how it is improving. In summary, the art teachers in the project saw assessment as a tool capable of helping art teachers to improve the quality of art education they provide.

The identification of evaluation criteria used by the art teachers, students of art, and artists produced some findings that also suggest further consideration. Among these groups, the purposes for conducting evaluation varied. As the purposes of the evaluation changed, so did the selection of evaluation criteria. Of special interest was the discussion of the differences among criteria selections by these groups. In general, art teacher criteria selections were primarily concerned with the development of the art product and were focused on the students' work. For example, art teachers placed greater emphasis on the elements of art, principles of design, composition, following directions, craftsmanship, and how well the work met the assignment objectives. In contrast, criteria selected by artists focused more heavily on their total development as an artist. Artists, for example, ranked originality, the degree of improvement or growth, development of a personal style, degree of change from previous work, and risk taking the highest. Obviously, artists felt they were being measured by the evidence found in the works of art produced. Artists, however, perceived their artwork in terms of how works related to their overall development as artists, rather than the specific growth any single work of art exhibited. One further difference between the art teachers and the artists was that art teachers ranked the principles of design and elements of art as the first criteria for assessing students' work, whereas artists ranked the principles tenth and the elements ninth.

Student rankings of these criteria were even lower, ranking the principles of design 16th and 13th in evaluating works made in school or at home. Students ranked the elements of art 1st for evaluating work they made in school and 4th for works made at home. Clearly, the emphasis art teachers placed on this criterion was at odds with the importance artists and students of art placed on it. Other examples of discrepancies occurred among the priorities of evaluation criteria used by art teachers, students of art, and artists. These included personal expression, experimentation or risk taking, and improvement or growth. This suggests a number of curriculum, instruction, and assessment issues those in higher education and art teachers in the field should consider. Art teachers and those who educate preservice art teachers need to ask themselves how the purposes of their assessments match the need to evaluate the ongoing artistic development of their students. Because of the pressures of accountability, art teachers might have difficulties in deciding whether art product quality is of greater importance than the overall artistic development of their students as exhibited in the total curriculum. Why increased cognitive development of student art knowledge and skills may not always be found in works of art is a question worthy of further consideration.

In a related issue, if assessment in art education is to shift increasingly more toward forms of authentic assessment that more accurately reflect measures used by artists, it follows that art teachers need to use authentic criteria in such a way that they reflect not only the criteria used by artists, but also the priorities given to such criteria by the artists. The issue of employing assessment measures utilized by artists that are not compatible with the priorities of artists would seem to defeat the purpose for using authentic assessments in the first place. This suggests that the purposes of assessment for art teachers differ from those of artists. If art teachers are equally concerned with the quality of their students' work and the overall artistic development of their students, then the ranking of evaluation criteria between art teachers and artists should be more in agreement. Rethinking the evaluation criteria selection process suggests substantial changes in the ways art teachers assess their students' work and, more significantly, for what purposes they assess that work.

The Electronic Portfolio Alternative

This assessment project was designed to investigate alternative models for assessment in the visual arts for uses at both the K–12 and university levels. Although student portfolios can be used as a means for documenting student performance over time, they also have their shortcomings. This is because they lack other forms of documentation and require the storage of drawings and three-dimensional works, such as sculpture or ceramics, over time. This has proven to be cumbersome in already overcrowded classrooms and has caused many teachers to stop using the standard portfolio because of the logistics of collecting artworks. Traditional photography can also be used effectively by the teacher to document art production over time, but it, too, is cumbersome. The sophistication of today's photographic processing and technology, especially through digital imaging that records images electronically on disks rather than on film, has now been proven to be a viable alternative to traditional methods for the storage and retrieval of visual images. This avoids the necessity of having to store all the original works of every student in order to have a permanent record of the students' progress over time.

The electronic portfolio study tested the feasibility of using different electronic formats for the development of portfolios at the elementary, secondary, and undergraduate college levels. The results of the study suggest that a number of important generalizations can be made about using electronic data collection methods and existing software programs to collect, organize, analyze, interpret, and assess student performance in the studio arts.

The results of the experiments using electronic portfolios suggest:

1. Elementary, secondary, and college students at all levels are able to use the Madeja visual modeling system to organize and collect data electronically. Even the most limited computer learner can be taught to use the various procedures outlined in the case studies in Chapter 6.
2. Older students, when first introduced to the electronic portfolio, thought that it would be an imposition to create an electronic portfolio. Elementary students, in contrast, were excited and enthusiastic about using digital cameras and scanners to record their

work. They eventually became proficient at systematically recording their work into formats created by the teacher as a database of their portfolio and soon became teacher-mentors to one another. The negative response in the beginning of the experiment on the part of some older students soon changed. Their attitudes toward creating electronic portfolios became positive because they saw the advantage of using them to record their accomplishments not only to view their own work, but also to see their progress in artistic development.

3. High school teachers also were initially resistant to this process because of a perceived time commitment. The electronic portfolio, when offered as an option for project teachers, resulted in roughly one half of them choosing to experiment in some way with the electronic portfolio. Many teachers even continued using them after the project ended, through developing other electronic formats for portfolios. What this suggests is that we can demonstrate the effectiveness of using electronic technologies for recording images and provide teachers with enough information for them to see their value as an assessment device. The study provided numerous models for electronic portfolios that can now be disseminated to teachers and demonstrate their use as assessment devices. This project can now be used to make the case that electronic portfolios can be a viable alternative to the traditional testing programs now being developed at the state level.

4. The electronic case studies presented in this study further demonstrate that expressive learning can be measured in ways other than those used in traditional testing programs. A need exists to develop viable alternatives for assessing student progress that relates more directly to what students learn in the art disciplines. Although a standardized state-wide testing program can be used as an indicator of student progress in specifically targeted content areas such as reading and mathematics, it should not be used as the only measure of student progress over time.

5. Expressive learning can be quantified. This study of school electronic portfolios has demonstrated that creative or expressive activities in the visual arts can be quantified. The study concludes that the process is generalizable and can apply at any level of instruction, starting in elementary grades and continuing through graduate education.

6. Art teachers are a valuable part of the assessment process and are the best judges of artistic merit and artistic quality of student artwork. This was demonstrated in the portfolio study (Appendix F) by the overwhelming agreement among judges at the $P = .01$ level on the quality of the artworks. The electronic portfolio case studies also demonstrate that students can be part of the assessment process and provide valuable evidence of what they have learned by creating electronic portfolios. Furthermore, at the elementary level, traditional grading practices can be integrated into the electronic portfolio design to be used as an assessment device and a record of student progress.

7. The lack of any agreement on a standardized curriculum in the visual arts continues to be a major problem that the art education field faces. Surveys indicate that there is

some common agreement on art content at the high school level. However, the lack of any standardization of the basal programs in K-8 is still a major problem in designing alternative instruments for assessing student progress. Visual arts testing programs now affect only about 25% of the states and most have little relevance to what is being taught in the art curriculum. This study demonstrates that student art assessment can be based on what is actually being taught in the classroom and also relate to state and national goals.

Recommendations for Further Study

Because the participants in the study came from different schools, it is suggested that the study be replicated with art teachers in a single school or within schools with similar school populations. At the secondary level, this could be accomplished through the study of several classes in a large high school or, at the elementary level, using classrooms from schools with similar populations. The expected outcome of the study would be to see how student performances vary among the same or similar school settings.

An effort also should be made to replicate the study in other areas of the U.S. using randomly selected school populations that could confirm the generalizability of the project's findings in different settings. This study would investigate the effects of involving other school populations, different individuals conducting the assessments, and different training activities as a means to increase the generalizability of research plans.

Another possible study would be to use other approaches to authentic assessment, including the use of different rubrics, teacher logs, teacher-constructed tests measuring content knowledge, and approaches to student self-evaluation. Such measures could further confirm or strengthen the predictability of the project's performance rubrics and also provide measures to better assess which additional forms of art classroom performance need to be considered.

An attempt also should be made to develop a system-wide assessment plan using some or all of the procedures used in this study in order to test the feasibility of a system-wide art performance assessment. This should include the development of sampling techniques that could be used to accurately assess the school district's art program without assessing every child at every level over 12 years of schooling. This effort should include the use of electronic portfolios designed to provide longitudinal studies of student progress over 12 years of schooling in art.

There also is a need to study what kind of teacher support and training is the most useful and has the greatest impact on the teacher and the students' arts performances. This study suggests, but does not confirm, that studio and curriculum training does have a positive impact on teacher and student behaviors. The study also includes findings that studio practice, without appropriate teaching methods on how to apply these strategies in the classroom, might not be as effective in improving student performance as instruction that combines studio and teaching methods. The effects of the training on the teacher and on the student also could be experimentally investigated with respect to the effectiveness of different approaches to studio training on the teacher and the students' performance.

Because the national standards and most state curricula recommend additional content in art history, aesthetics, and art criticism, additional rubrics and evaluation systems should be developed and tested to measure achievement in these areas of art learning. A number of states now are developing state assessments in

6 CONCLUSIONS AND RECOMMENDATIONS

visual arts. Studies of state assessment practices, such as the study conducted by Sabol (1994), should be conducted to identify practices, purposes, rationales, types, and content of state assessment. Modeling assessments that use the findings of such studies better enable art teachers to evaluate and modify assessment practices to become more compatible with assessment used by states.

The preservice training of art teachers must change in order for it to maintain pace with developments in public schools. A study of preservice assessment training of art teachers, including assessment courses and practical experience in applying assessments in classroom settings, will help teachers to become more effective in assessing art learning. Further research also is needed to identify professional development needs in assessment that should be used to educate teachers. Art teachers need specialized professional development opportunities for assessment training. We also need to know what professional development opportunities in assessment exist, what kinds of support local school districts, state departments of education, state art education associations, national art education associations, art museums, and other agencies provide for art teachers, and how art teachers can take advantage of these opportunities.

References

Sabol, F. R. (1994). A critical examination of visual arts achievement tests from state departments of education in the United States. Dissertation Abstracts International, #56 (2A), 9518525 (University Microfilms No. 5602A)

Sabol, F. R. (1998a). Needs assessment and identification of urban art teachers in the western region of the National Art Education Association. Reston, VA: The National Art Education Foundation.

Sabol, F. R. (1998b). What are we testing?: Content analysis of state visual arts achievement tests. Visual Arts Research, 24, 1–12

Sabol, F. R. (1999). Needs assessment and identification of rural art teachers in the western region of the National Art Education Association. Reston, VA: The National Art Education Foundation.

Sabol, F. R. (2001). Reaching out to rural and urban art teachers in the western region of the National Art Education Association: Needs assessment and identification of new members. Reston, VA: National Art Education Foundation.

Sabol, F. R., & Bensur, B. (2000, April). What attitudes do art teachers hold about assessment in art education? Paper presented at the national convention of the National Art Education Association, Los Angeles, CA.

Appendix A
Art Teachers' Studio Product Evaluation Criteria (N = 59)

Criterion	f	%
Elements of art	56	94.9
Principles of design	56	94.9
Composition or use of space	56	94.6
Creativity	56	94.9
Followed directions	51	86.4
Technical skill or craftsmanship	51	86.4
Work meets assignment objectives	51	86.4
Personal expression	49	83.1
Completed processes correctly	48	81.4
Attention to detail	47	79.7
Originality	47	79.7
Improvement or growth	46	78.0
Representation of space or distance	44	74.6
Knowledge of concepts	43	72.9
Work matches its intent	43	72.9
Experimentation or risk taking	40	67.8
Sophistication of theme or idea	40	67.8
Safe use of materials and equipment	38	64.4
Appropriateness of theme	37	62.7
Cognitive processes	37	62.7
Visual accuracy	33	55.9
Use of style	29	49.2
Art historical content	24	45.8
Other	3	5.1

Appendix B
Student Performance Criteria (N = 59)

Criterion	f	%
Effort	54	91.5
Problem-solving ability	53	89.8
Improvement or growth	48	81.4
Classroom behavior	44	74.6
Self-motivation or initiative	44	74.6
Turning in assignment on time	42	71.2
Use of previous knowledge	42	71.2
Reflection or thoughtfulness (metacognition)	40	67.8
Critical thinking	39	66.1
Decision making	39	66.1
Synthesis of ideas	35	59.3
Following clean-up procedures	34	57.6
Problem identification	32	54.2
Evaluation of ideas	29	49.2
Reasoning or use of logic	28	47.5
Analytical ability	26	44.1
Attendance	24	40.7
Behavior in groups	24	40.7
Other	1	1.7

Appendix C

At School: Students' Studio Product Evaluation Criteria (N = 472)

Criterion	f	%
How well I used the elements of art	349	73.9
My skill with art materials	329	69.7
If I followed the teacher's directions	315	66.7
How well I showed details in my work	312	66.1
Neatness	301	63.8
How well I showed my ideas in the work	290	61.4
If I experimented or tried to make it different or unique	267	56.6
How well I filled space	264	55.9
If I felt I learned something new	261	55.3
If my idea was new or different from my other ideas	248	52.5
If I did everything the way I wanted it done. It pleased me.	224	47.5
If I did what I thought the teacher wanted	223	47.2
If the work showed what I know	221	46.8
How much this work made me think	218	46.2
If I used materials and equipment safely	217	46.0
Use of principles of design	202	42.8
If I solved a problem well	184	39.0
Something else	50	10.6

Appendix D
At Home: Students' Studio Product Evaluation Criteria (n = 380)

Criterion	f	%
My skill with art materials	245	64.5
If I did everything the way I wanted it done it pleased me.	236	62.1
Neatness	231	60.8
How well I used the elements of art	229	60.3
How well I showed details in my work	226	59.5
How well I showed my ideas in the work	225	59.2
How well I filled space	190	50.0
If I experimented or tried to make it different or unique	188	49.5
If my idea was new or different from my other ideas	179	47.1
If I felt I learned something new	169	44.5
How much this work made me think	166	43.7
If the work showed what I know	164	43.2
Use of principles of design	156	41.1
If I used materials and equipment safely	131	34.5
If I solved a problem well	119	31.3
Something else	31	8.2

Appendix E
Artists' Studio Product Evaluation Criteria (N = 50)

Criterion	f	%
Originality	45	90.0
Degree of improvement or growth	43	86.0
Composition	42	84.0
Development of personal style, expression, or aesthetic	40	80.0
Technical skill with media	40	80.0
Degree of change from previous work or risk taking	40	80.0
Successful communication of ideas	38	76.0
Effective use of the principles of design	30	60.0
Effective use of the elements of art	29	58.0
Potential to expand the field of art	23	46.0
Degree the work matches the original intent	23	46.0
Degree of similarity with previous work	13	26.0
Degree the work matches the needs of exhibitions or galleries	10	20.0
Degree the work matches requirements of grants or commissions	10	20.0
Degree the work will be accepted by the public	9	18.0
Degree the work matches the need of a patron or client	8	16.0
Other	3	6.0

Appendix F

Summary of Student Portfolio Findings

Before reporting the analysis of the data on the student portfolio assessments, it should be kept in mind that this effort was not an experimental study where experimental and control groups were compared. It is not, therefore, possible to report empirically verified evidence that all the research goals were confirmed, even if the numbers tend to support all four of the research claims that the process does support the quantification of expressive behaviors, that there was a high level of interrater reliability among teachers scoring the pretest and posttest portfolios, that the scores were normally distributed, and that gains in mean scores were unevenly distributed among student scoring in both the higher and lower performance categories.

Neither will the report present the actual mean scores for the students, school districts, and project sites in order to protect the privacy of the data and not misrepresent the goals of authentic assessment, which are not about reporting failures or successes, but rather about how children, teachers, schools, and school districts can do a better job of educating students.

Although data from two four-works portfolios from nearly 1,000 students in 51 classrooms from 15 school districts were analyzed, in some cases the sample was too small to be absolutely certain about some of the conclusions or suggestions reported. The most important question to be answered was whether there was a high level of interrater reliability among the three different raters scoring each portfolio. These comparisons were reported in two ways: A-1, the initial scoring of the pre-test portfolio, and B-1, B-2, an assessment comparing the pretest portfolio and the posttest portfolio as one group. Although the same group adjudicated the A-1, B-1, and B-2 adjudications, the mean score gains in the B-1, B-2 adjudications were greater than between the A-1 and B-2 comparisons. Scores on the pretest portfolios scored separately tended to be higher than when they were later mixed and blind scored in the B-1, B-2 comparisons.

Table F1 shows the interrater reliability as measured by the Spearman's rho coefficient for the correlation between the mean scores provided by the raters in A-1 and B-1, B-2 assessments for all schools in Florida and Indiana. This table reveals all the correlation coefficients were medium to low, but all were significant. The correlations between A-1 and B-2 were the lowest and those between B-1 and B-2 were the highest. The B-1, B-2 comparisons suggest that in only 1% of the cases is it possible that the mean scores for the pre- and posttest differ,which suggests an extremely high level of agreement among the raters in the B-1, B-2 pre- and posttest comparisons.

Table F1
Correlation between score means of
group of raters (A1, B1, and B2):
N = 973.

Correlation Between Score Means of
Group of Raters (A1, B1 and B2)
N=973

	Score Means for Group A1 Raters	Score Means for Group B1 Raters	Score Means for Group B2 Raters
Score Means for Group A1 Raters	1		
Score Means for Group B1 Raters	.552**	1	
Score Means for Group B2 Raters	.345**	.442**	1

** Correlation is significant at the .01 level (2-tailed).

Table F2 answers the question of whether the rater scores for a given classroom were normally distributed and whether there was sufficient score spread in order to determine whether the test discriminated among the portfolio scores. The box plots depicting the distributions of scores in the pretest (A-1) and B-1, B-2 pre- and posttest comparisons reveal the score spread for A-1 as being smaller than in the B-1, B-2 comparisons, with the scores in the B-2 pretest having greater range and a more normal distribution than either A-1 or B-2, and a greater number of high scores in B-2. This suggests that the test is more discriminatory when comparing the B-1 and B-2 portfolios.

Table F2
Box plots depicting the distributions of raters' score
means on the pretest (A1, (B1) and posttest (B2).

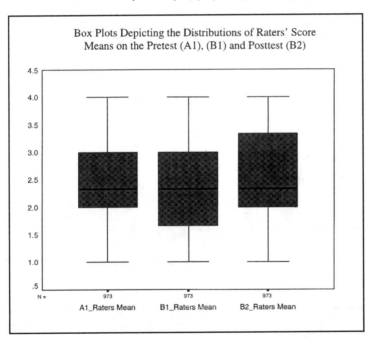

The question of whether there was an improvement in the group mean for each school following the training of the teachers cannot be statistically confirmed, but gains in the class mean scores occurred in 33 of the 52 schools. Gains in mean scores comparing B-2 and A-1 occurred in four other schools, which suggests at least some mean score gains in 71% of the schools. On a 4-point scale, gains ranged from 1.0, a

25% gain, to as little as .10, which suggests little if any gain. In 16 schools the mean class score increased by more than 50%. In 11 schools, or about 30% of the schools, mean scores in the pre- and posttest showed a decline. These ranged from declines as low as .03 points to .50 points, with nearly half being less than .1 points. It should be noted that the decline in the mean score for a given class does not mean that the student performance decreased from what it was in the beginning, but rather that lower student scores are more likely to occur when compared to a significant number of students showing significant gains.

To determine if the losses or gains in class mean performances were significant the Wilcoxon Signed Ranks test, a nonparametric test to compare two related samples, was used. The results were significant at the .05 level of confidence, with 19 of the 51 schools significantly positive or negative. Table F3 reveals the gain or loss for the 51 schools with .00 as the mean score. The table also reveals that 36 of the 51 classrooms improved over time.

Table F3
Gain (B2-B1) for all schools.

Gain (B2-B1) for all schools

Table F4 shows whether the gain in mean scores occurred evenly at all grade levels. The results suggested that the greatest gain occurred at the 6–8 grade levels, somewhat less at the 1–3 grade levels, and much less in the 9–12 and 4–5 grade levels, with the smallest gains occurring in grades 4 and 5.

Table F4
Gains in mean scores by grade levels.

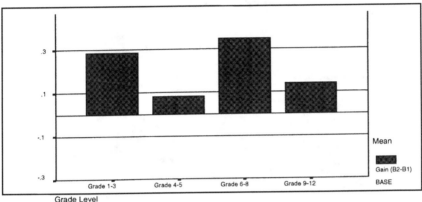

Grade Level

As to whether some of the 51 schools in Florida, Indiana, and Illinois revealed greater student gains than others, this appeared to be the case. The gains in Illinois, where no studio interventions were offered, revealed little or no gain. Interestingly, in one of the Indiana districts where teachers did participate in the studio workshops, there was actually a loss in the mean scores. Among the districts that showed gains, the mean score gain ranged from .15 to .35 on a 4-point scale.

The final question was whether lower and higher performing students with differing art ability levels show the same gains in student performance. Table F5 revealed the gains and losses in mean scores for the 51 schools according to the scores of higher and lower performing students, with the mean score for each classroom being considered the base line 0. Increases are revealed in scores above the 0 level and decreases are shown below the 0 level. The table suggests that, whereas less than half of the higher achieving students improved in their scores, 85% of low-performing students improved their scores.

Table F5
Gains and losses in mean scores for higher and lower achieving students in all schools.

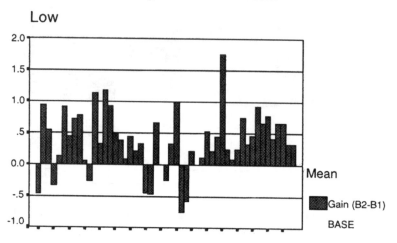

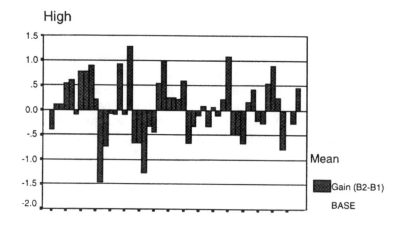

Table F6, which reveals the gains among high- and low-performing students by grade level, suggests these gains as not being evenly distributed. The table suggests lower performing students, as measured on B-1, improve at all levels, with higher performing students on B-1 showing at least some improvement at all levels except grades 4 through 6.

Table F6
Gain for high vs. low performing students (B2-B1) by grades.

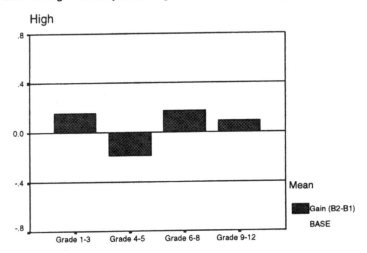

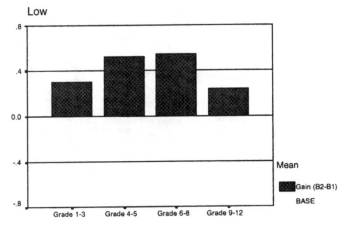

Author Index

Subject Index

201